Sisters in Arms

COURAGEOUS WOMEN
OF THE REFORMATION

"The Reformation comes alive with these stories of faith, adventure and love. The eight women featured in these stories were not only heroes, but flesh-and-blood humans who had fears and excitement and doubts and temptations. They were not perfect, but the reader is touched and inspired by their growing faith and their willingness to suffer for it.

"New author Sukeshinie Goonatilleke has made these leaders of the Reformation jump from the page and into our hearts. The historical details are clear and help with our education, but it is the humanity of each of these women that stands out. Their loves, fears and faith help the reader to both understand the past and have sympathy for it.

"For all who see themselves as children of the Reformation, it is vital to learn about the women who helped lead this movement. *Sisters in Arms* highlights many of the women heroes of the faith—using both deep historical detail and exciting, action-packed stories. As I read these stories, the Protestant leadership emerged as fully human, with emotions and flaws just like me. What an inspiration!"

—**Dr Lisa Clark Diller**, Professor of History,
    Southern Adventist University.

Sisters in Arms

COURAGEOUS WOMEN
OF THE REFORMATION

SUKESHINIE
GOONATILLEKE

SIGNS
PUBLISHING®
Established 1885

The author assumes full responsibility for the accuracy of all facts and
quotations cited in this book.

All Bible quotations are taken from the Holy Bible, King James Version.

Proudly published and printed in Australia by
Signs Publishing
Warburton, Victoria.

This book was
Edited by Lauren Webb
Proofread by Lachlan Garland
Cover design by Shane Winfield
Cover images by D Keine, Getty Images/Shutterstock
Typeset in Berkeley Book 11.5/15 pt

ISBN (print edition) 978 1 922373 24 3
ISBN (ebook edition) 978 1 922373 25 0

For Elyse and Carys

"Favour is deceitful, and beauty is vain:
but a woman that feareth the Lord, she shall be praised."
—Proverbs 31:30

Contents

Foreword

When we think of the Reformation we often think of the great men who started the movement. Men like Martin Luther, William Tyndale and John Calvin. Unfortunately, the women who were a part of this movement are often overlooked.

This book provides a fascinating insight into the lives of eight female heroes of the Reformation. Their stories are sure to resonate with people from various backgrounds and all walks of life. You will find that the women in this book are from various ranks and segments of society, from the highest to the lowest, yet their faith and commitment to God is a single unifying thread that runs through the book and binds their experience to ours.

Sometimes it is easy to read about the great reformers and wonder how we could ever accomplish anything as grand or heroic as they did. But when you read the story of Marie Durand, who at the age of nineteen took such a decisive stand for God, you cannot help but be inspired. She was not a theologian, pastor or teacher, but her unwavering commitment to God's Word through thirty-eight years of imprisonment speaks to each of us.

Each of these women faced enormous tests and overcame them. As you read this book you will be drawn into the experience of each character. The stories are so vivid and personal that they bring the characters to life, making each of them both relatable and personable.

Some of these women broke with tradition and blazed a new trail for those who would come after them, like Katharina von Bora, who as the wife of Martin Luther, set an example for other wives of faith. Then there are those like Queen Katherine Parr and Louise de Coligny, who lived in royal courts and rubbed shoulders with the elite of society, yet still maintained their faith in God.

These stories are sure to captivate, enrich, motivate and encourage you as you attempt to navigate the challenges you face, challenges that might seem different on the surface but at their core are very much the same: issues of faithfulness to God, commitment to His Word and deeper education in spiritual things.

In many ways, this book is a fruit of the many hours that Sukeshinie volunteered researching and writing articles for the Lineage Journey website. Lineage is an educational media ministry that creates resources to teach young people about church history. Sukeshinie came on board shortly after the ministry launched in 2017. Since then, she has written more than 150 articles and blogs for the website, which have been a blessing to countless people around the world. Many of those articles formed the basis for the stories that you will find in this book.

I pray that as you read this book and stand on the shoulders of these spiritual giants, you will be able to look to their examples of faith and courage to guide you no matter what you face in the future.

Adam Ramdin
Executive Producer, Lineage Journey
Youth Director, North England Conference of Seventh-day Adventists

Preface

The Reformation was the zeitgeist of the 16th century. More than any other social or political event during that period, the Reformation made the most significant impact on every facet of life. The movement was led by giants—juggernauts of spiritual and intellectual accomplishment who were unafraid to stand up and fearlessly proclaim God's Word.

Together, they introduced people to the truth of justification by faith, the great cornerstone of Christianity, and placed the Bible in the hands of a populace that had, up to that point, been largely ignorant of what it contained. They also came to recognise the importance of religious liberty. The great German reformer Martin Luther summarised it best when he stood before the emperor at the Diet of Worms and boldly declared, "My conscience is captive to the Word of God."

The idea that an individual's conscience was free and could be directed as that individual chose was foreign to the people of early modern Europe. As foreign was the idea that a man or woman's conscience could and should be wholly captive to the Word of God. The Reformation changed that. But a deeper study of the Reformation reveals something else—that history was shaped as much by faithful women as it was by faithful men.

As much as men like Luther, Calvin and Zwingli revolutionised their world and ours, there were also remarkable women who worked in a similar fashion and accomplished significant feats in their own right.

These women came from every walk of life. Like many of us, they were wives, mothers, sisters, daughters and friends. But they were also heads of state, writers, activists, poets and scholars. They were women who helped shape not only their homes and families but also their communities and nations. This book is dedicated to telling their stories.

The idea for this book first came to me when I was doing a series of blog posts on women of the Reformation for Women's History Month in March, 2018. The more I dug into the lives of the women of the Reformation, the more I began to see common threads that bound them, as well as an amazing array of differences that made them stand apart as individuals.

Of all the women I read about, the eight women included in this book made the greatest impact on me. In many ways, these women were flawed and moulded by the social norms of their times, yet they demonstrated a dauntless commitment to God's Word that led them to defy social biases and traditions. They were deeply human and at the same time deeply spiritual as well. They are women of the German, French and English Reformations, and their stories are grouped together in this book by geographical region and then by chronology. I have tried to follow the historical narrative as closely as possible, though I have exercised some artistic licence in places. My goal overall was to be as true to these women and their stories as possible, because there is something powerful about telling true stories. I believe they can capture the imagination as thoroughly as fiction.

These women were not afraid to follow their consciences and make hard choices, even at great cost to themselves. Their lives are described in Revelation 12:11: "And they overcame him by the blood of the Lamb, and by the word of their testimony; and they loved not their lives unto the death." It was this that drew me to them.

Men who fought together on the front lines of history's great wars are often referred to as "brothers in arms." Commitment to a common goal and willingness to make enormous sacrifices in the pursuit of it bound these men together inextricably in a brotherhood that was often stronger than any blood tie.

Similarly, these women, though in some cases separated by time and space, chose to pursue a common goal at great personal cost.

Though they did not take up physical arms, they took up the sword of the Spirit, which is the Word of God, and the shield of faith and went to war against formidable forces of spiritual darkness. This bound them together. This made them sisters in arms. And those of us who pursue a similar commitment to God's Word regardless of the ensuing costs are part of that community as well. We too are brothers and sisters in arms, to each other and also to them.

As you read this book, I hope you are as deeply moved and inspired by the lives of these amazing women as I have been. I pray that they not only inspire you but that they also challenge you to examine your own commitment to God's Word, so that you too can experience the unique joy of fellowship with Jesus that they each treasured.

Sukeshinie Goonatilleke
September, 2020

1

Katharina von Bora

RUNAWAY

Nimbschen, The Holy Roman Empire of the German Nation
April 4, 1523

The stillness of the night is pierced by loud rattling and the pounding of hooves. We all tense at the sound, wondering if it is the man we have been waiting for. We are nervous and skittish, huddled around the thick garden door leading out into the lane beyond.

Beside me, Veronika leans towards Margaret. "Do you think it is him?" she whispers.

Margaret presses her face against the rough wooden door and peers out into darkness. "It could be," she replies.

"Well, if it is him then why must he make such a racket? We will be caught before we even leave the convent, Margaret!" Elsa complains. Margaret turns and silences her with a glare.

"Could he not be more discreet?" Ava agrees, shooting Margaret a glare of her own. This is all Margaret's doing. She is the one who has written to Brother Martin for help.

"He has come to help us and frankly we should be grateful that anyone has come at all," Margaret tells us imperiously.

The moon is high tonight and the countryside is awash with pale silvery light. It is not the best night for our escape, but beggars can't be choosers and tonight we are beggars. The rattling gets louder and I nudge Margaret out of the way to peek around the corner of the garden door at the approaching wagon.

"I pray Sister von Haubitz is soundly asleep," Elsa says right beside my ear. "She will hang us out to dry like sheets in the wind if she catches us."

"Shhh," Veronika whispers. "Be quiet all of you! Your whispering alone is going to wake the Abbess."

The rattling comes to an abrupt halt and I hear the soft nickering of horses not far from where we stand. We wait, listening for the signal that will confirm that this is indeed the man we have been waiting for. Then we hear it, a soft piercing whistle, once, twice, three times.

"It's him," Margaret says, and a ripple of excitement goes through the small knot of young women gathered around the garden door.

"Go see if it's really him, Katie," Veronika prompts, nudging me forward. I look over at Margaret, who nods her agreement.

"Why me?" I ask bewildered. "Shouldn't you be going?"

Margaret shrugs. "You're the only one of us who isn't afraid of anything," she says mildly. "Now go on, we don't have all night!"

Sighing, I slide through the gate and out into the open country lane. I spot him in the shadow of the wall to my left and make my way over, keeping out of the moonlight.

"Herr Koppe?" I whisper, when I am close enough.

"Yes," he whispers back, and I hear the creak of wood as he steps down from the driver's seat and comes to meet me by the horses' heads. Leonhard Koppe is known to us, but unfortunately not for his intellect.

"I am Katie…Katharina," I say, suddenly shy that I, a nun, am having a secret rendezvous with a strange man outside the walls of my abbey in the middle of the night.

"Fraulein Katharina," he greets me formally. "Are the other sisters ready?"

"Yes," I reply, my eyes shifting to the rickety cart. "You will transport us in this…wagon?"

"Uh, yes." He scratches the back of his neck. "Dr Luther suggested that a wagon might be the most effective...uh...means of escape. How many of you are there?"

"There are twelve of us," I say, as I eye the vehicle. He nods and I see that his face is serene, as if smuggling nuns out of a convent in the dead of night were an everyday occurrence. "This could very well be a fool's errand," I blurt out before I can stop myself.

"Yes," he concedes, "but we will not know unless we try."

It is not like you have many other options, Katie, I think. Then I nod. "I will get the others," I tell him and hurry back to the garden door.

Quietly, I gather my sisters and we slip out into the lane in a huddle, melting into the shadows like thieves in the night. We gather around the wagon and when I glance up to measure Herr Koppe's reaction, I see that his usually calm face is showing signs of concern.

"Well?" Margaret snaps impatiently, taking in his dazed expression. It is too late for regrets now. "Where do you want us?"

"What do you want us to do?" Elsa repeats.

Herr Koppe stares at us for a long moment, then mutters, "I have brought fish barrels."

"Fish barrels?" Veronika asks. "Whatever for?"

"I thought..." he shifts and rubs the back of his neck, "I thought you might travel in them."

"Travel in fish barrels?" Ava repeats, looking at him like he has lost his mind. "How big are they?"

He motions for us to come around to the back of the wagon and look, and we follow him, a soft ripple of indignation passing between us.

"Fish barrels?"

"Has he gone mad?"

"Perhaps they are larger than we expect?"

"Humph...I doubt it."

"*Shhh*," Margaret hisses.

I jump in then, hoping to placate everyone, "The man has been good enough to risk his neck and find a way to conceal us. The least we can do is show some gratitude."

"Let's see how grateful you are when you have to sit inside a stinking fish barrel, Katie von Bora," Veronika murmurs. I sigh, knowing that she's right.

The barrels are squat wooden receptacles with bands of iron wrapped around their bulging middles. "Here they are," Herr Koppe says, looking sheepish.

Gathering up my skirt in one hand, I hitch my foot into the spokes of the wheels and awkwardly squeeze between two barrels and onto the wagon bed. Cautiously, I peer into a barrel. In the moonlight, I see a sludge of fish entrails lining the bottom and the stench of rotting fish hits me. I rear back wrinkling my nose.

"What is it?" Margaret whispers, and I turn to see her climbing up into the wagon behind me. She peers into a barrel and I see her face blanch. We exchange a look and then glance at Herr Koppe, whose face has resumed its placid expression. I turn back to the fish barrel and hitch my leg over the rim, struggling a little to get inside.

Before long, all twelve of us are crammed into the wretched fish barrels, our knees jammed against our chests and the stench of rotting fish seeping into our skins. The sludge of old fish entrails is damp and cold beneath me. An involuntary shudder passes through my body at the thought.

"Even if I wash for a thousand years, this stink will never come out of my skin," I hear Elsa whisper hoarsely from the next barrel.

When we are settled, Herr Koppe takes the reins and we begin our journey. The road is rough and uneven and the wagon bounces hard. Soon my entire body is rattling and I clamp my jaw tight until it aches. *Two days of this*, I think. *Two whole days of rattling and jolting in this stinking brew of fish*. I close my eyes, reminding myself of why we are doing this, how it all started and why it is worth it.

Summer, 1519

My favourite place in the whole convent is the library. I love the musty smell of books and ink and the scarred tables lining the stone room. I am reading a book on canonical law, my brow furrowed as I take in the concept of *extra ecclesiam nulla salus*—there is no salvation outside the church—when a sound behind me makes me look up. It is Veronika, eyes wide, a small sheaf of bound papers clutched in her hand.

"What is it?" I ask, shutting the heavy book. "What's happened?"

She sinks into the chair beside me and casts a glance around the room. There are a few other sisters in the library quietly reading.

"Veronika," I say, as I follow her gaze. "What's . . ."

"Shhh," she presses a finger against her lips. "I have just received a pamphlet," she says, her voice so low I have to lean almost against her mouth to hear her.

"From where?" I ask, my brow furrowing again. Ever since this monk Martin Luther commenced his rampage, we have been instructed to be very careful about the kind of literature we accept.

"From my uncle," she says, looking at the papers in her hand.

"The prior at the monastery in Grimma?" I lean back, my shoulders sagging in relief. If she has a book from her uncle the monk, then we have nothing to worry about. "So, what is the problem?" I ask, forgetting to whisper.

"*Katie!*" she hisses. "*Keep your voice down!*"

"What on earth for?" I ask, though I oblige. "If your Uncle Wolfgang sent you a book, it can hardly be contraband."

"That's just it," she whispers, placing the papers on top of my book. "He has sent me a pamphlet written by Martin Luther."

"What?" I glance down at the pamphlet, slowly taking in the title: "Lessons on the Epistle of Paul to the Romans." It appears to be a collection of sermons. I quickly take the pamphlet and slide it under my book, my eyes darting around the room. The other sisters seem oblivious to us.

"He sent me a letter," Veronika continues. "He says that Brother Martin was at the priory in Grimma a few weeks ago and preached to the brothers there. He says he believes every word Brother Martin preaches, Katie. He has sent us this collection of sermons so that we can study what he teaches for ourselves."

I am too shocked to speak. I stare at her, my mouth opening and closing like a fish.

"Well?" she demands. "Say something!"

"It is heresy," I finally choke out. "Surely your uncle knows how dangerous this is?"

"He does not think it is heresy," she says, and I shake my head.

"Then he is a heretic himself."

"Katie! How can you say something is heretical until you have taken the time to study it?"

"Because the Abbess has told me that anything that comes out of the mouth of Martin Luther is heresy," I retort.

"And that is enough for you?" she challenges.

"Is it not enough for you?" I reply hotly.

"You would throw out everything he says just because the Abbess says so? I never would have thought you would be so . . ." she pauses, searching for the right word.

"So what?" I ask dryly, then I cut her off with a dismissive wave of my hand. "Don't try to manipulate me, Veronika. I do not like to invite trouble."

"What if it is trouble worth inviting?" she replies, raising her eyebrows.

I sigh in exasperation. "So what will you do with this?" I ask, motioning towards the pamphlet still in my lap.

"We will study it," she says.

"Who is we?" I ask.

"Margaret von Staupitz and Ava von Schonfeld, Elsa and myself. We plan to meet in my room tonight after the lights are out. Please Katie, say you will come."

"Veronika, this is madness. Who knows what will happen to us if we are caught? I heard that Martin Luther disputed with Dr Eck at Leipzig just last month. The entire church is in an uproar about this." I lean closer and whisper in her ear. "They might even burn him as a heretic. And then where will we be? What will they do to us if we are caught reading his work?"

She is silent for a moment. "He is using Erasmus' new translation of the New Testament, you know," she finally replies, as though she hasn't heard a single word I have said.

"What?"

"Erasmus of Rotterdam." She gives me an exasperated look. "You know who he is, Katie."

"Yes," I reply. "I know who Erasmus is, but what of it? Erasmus dedicated his new translation to the pope himself. I fail to see how it could propagate heresy."

"It's a different sort of translation, Katie. Everyone is saying it's...it's so refreshing."

"But surely the Holy Father would have come across any inconsistencies?" I say.

"Perhaps the Holy Father hasn't read it?" Veronika offers, biting her lip.

"*Veronika!*" I gasp.

"Well, I have heard say," she replies, her chin tilting up stubbornly, "that the Holy Father called the gospel a profitable fable." She leans back and studies me.

"That's nonsense," I say dismissively.

"Is it? We owe it to ourselves to see if there is any truth in what Brother Martin is saying. Come on, Katie! There is a copy of Erasmus' Bible here in the library. We can use it to check every reference Brother Martin makes in his pamphlet. There is nothing to lose, is there? If it is heresy like everyone says, then we can see for ourselves and be done with it, but if it is true, like my Uncle Wolfgang says it is, then how can we walk away from it?"

I sigh and shake my head. Veronika is right. "Alright," I say grudgingly. "I will come."

Her face breaks into a wide grin. "You will not regret it, Katie. I promise you won't!"

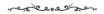

That night we meet in Veronika's room, huddled around her hard bed, a single tallow taper flickering on the small wooden stool nearby. There is an air of excitement in the room, coupled with tension. We read Brother Martin's pamphlet, flipping open Erasmus'

heavy translation of the New Testament and comparing it with Brother Martin's conclusions. We stay like that until we hear the low tolling of the bells summoning us for Lauds, the hour of mass just before dawn.

I glance up from the Bible, my eyes stinging with the strain of reading in dim candlelight. "We must go down for Lauds or they will wonder where we are." The others nod.

"I'll return the Bible to the library later," Veronika says.

None of us have slept a wink, but I doubt that we could have even if we had wanted to.

Adrenaline is pumping through my veins and I am wide awake as we enter the chapel and go through the motions of Lauds. I barely blink when I bow to the host or when I repeat the words. My mind goes back to the book I was reading when Veronika came to me, and the dogma that there is no salvation outside the church. My eyes narrow on the monstrance—an ornate case holding the consecrated host—on the altar before us, the great rood on the wall, and a thought hits me like a great boulder, shattering a hundred ideas I have cherished for so long. If Brother Martin *is* right, then salvation can be found outside the church but not outside of Christ.

The more we study, the more we are convinced that Brother Martin is right. We tear through the book of Romans, hanging on St Paul's every word. Salvation outside the church but not outside of Christ. Salvation *only* in Christ. When we come to the first verse of Romans Chapter 5, I hear the scaffolding of an entire system of belief begin to pull apart in my mind.

"Therefore being justified by faith, we have peace with God through our Lord Jesus Christ," Veronika reads quietly. She lifts her eyes from the page and looks around at us all. Justified by faith. Not by the sacraments or indulgences but by *faith*. It is an idea that is impossible to conceive. Too wide and high and deep to comprehend. Salvation by faith.

"If this is heresy, then I shall gladly be called a heretic," Ava says.

It is a reformation of ideas, of beliefs, of thoughts. A reformation of our very hearts. And once the fire has been kindled, it seems that nothing can stop the blaze. We study each night until we are exhausted and the Abbess, my aunt, remarks on it. Then we are more careful, studying in private during our free time in the library, only meeting once a week to discuss what we have learned together. I am like a woman possessed. The Word of God consumes my every waking thought and I want nothing else.

January, 1521

"They have excommunicated him."

I turn to stare at Margaret von Staupitz. "Who?" I ask. I am in the great hall, stacking logs into the crackling fire.

"*Who else?*" she hisses, grabbing my arm and propelling me into a small alcove in the gallery beyond.

"Dr Luther?" I ask, and she nods.

"My brother has written to me," she continues. "He says that Brother Martin took the papal bull of excommunication and burned it for all the world to see at the Elster Gate in Wittenberg."

I gape at her in shock. "Surely he would not defy the Holy Father in such a manner?" I whisper, scandalised.

Margaret's eyes are shining with a mixture of excitement and fear. "He did. His books have all been proscribed. They are to be burned and anyone found reading them condemned as a heretic."

At this, I feel a shiver race along my spine. We have been receiving his pamphlets regularly through Veronika's uncle. "Should we burn what we have?" I ask Margaret. "Have you talked with the others?"

"No, I have not talked to the others, but I think it might be wise to burn what we have. If we are caught handling them, there is no telling what might happen." She pauses and studies me. "You know that Brother Martin holds my brother Johann in high esteem," she says, and I nod. Margaret's brother is Dr Johann von Staupitz, and she has told us that he has had a great deal of influence over Brother Martin. "Johann fears that Brother Martin will be summoned to appear before the emperor soon."

"Will they burn him?" I ask, and Margaret nods.

"They will if they can find reason enough."

"We must be careful then," I tell Margaret. "Perhaps we should stop studying and...and just go back."

"Go back?" she interrupts me, incredulously. "Go back to what? Believing in indulgences and relics? Would you really do that, Katie?"

"He is causing a stir and...I am not certain that I want to be caught up in all of this."

"I had never pegged you for a coward, Katie von Bora," Margaret says.

I glare at her and raise my chin a notch, my eyes flashing fire. "I am no coward, Margaret von Staupitz," I bite back. "But neither am I a fool. If he has been excommunicated and proscribed by the Holy Father himself as a heretic, then we would do well to be wary of his teachings. Are you really ready to turn your back on the Holy Father and the church? Are you really ready to throw in your lot with a man as wild and as unstable as Brother Martin Luther? You yourself told me that he is often beset with bouts of melancholia. How do we know that he is even in his right mind?"

Margaret snorts in a most unladylike manner and waves her hand dismissively. "I do not pretend to know Brother Martin's state of mind, Katie, but I do know this: he speaks the truth. I have seen it with my own eyes and not just from his writings but from the Bible. He is right when he talks of *sola scriptura* and *sola fide* and *sola Christus*. Do you deny it?"

My shoulders sag under the weight of her words and I avert my eyes, studying the flagstones at my feet. I cannot deny it. Each particle of truth I have gleaned has been as sweet as honey in my mouth. "It is a high price to pay, Margaret," I say instead. "This is all I have ever known. I was gifted to the convent by my father at the age of five. I have grown up in the shelter of a cloister my whole life. Where would I go if I embraced this new doctrine openly? What would become of me? I would not know how to live out there. Would I marry? For no woman can remain unmarried in society. A woman who is not protected by the church needs the protection of a man." I shake my head. "I cannot even begin to comprehend what life would be like outside these walls."

Margaret's eyes soften and she lays a gentle hand on my arm. "God will lead you, Katie. One step at a time. But it is up to you to decide which path you will choose."

Summer, 1521

We hear about what has happened at the Diet of Worms from Margaret's brother Dr von Staupitz and from others. It seems that every peddler that stops at the convent has a different version of the same tale. They say that Dr Luther was greeted by adoring crowds at every city and village he travelled through, they say that Dr Luther has bested the emperor and the pope and all of the scholars in Christendom. They say that Dr Luther will set them free from papal indulgences and papal taxes and that now the peasants might raise their heads just a fraction.

We are dumb with shock. We cannot believe that he has had the gall to stand before the emperor and declare that he will not listen to popes or councils, because they have often contradicted themselves. We cannot believe that he has told them that his conscience is captive to the Word of God alone. We half expect the emperor to flay him alive while he is still at Worms, but instead the emperor honours Dr Luther's safe conduct and allows him to return to Wittenberg. But no sooner has he left than the emperor issues the Edict of Worms, damning Martin Luther as a heretic and calling for his immediate arrest.

It forces us all to count the cost. For now Brother Martin is no longer a raving monk of questionable mental capability. He is a man hunted for his life, a man preaching against the Holy Father and the church, and any man, or woman, who is foolish enough to follow him will be as hunted and reviled as he is. I am reticent to attend our regular Bible study sessions. Fear keeps me away. Night after night I go into the little chapel at the convent and kneel on the flagstones, pleading with God for guidance, for help. I do not think I have prayed this way before, but now I find that I have nowhere else to turn. The Word of God has become precious to me, and yet it is also like a great sword, slashing at the cables that hold me to the only

11

anchor I have known all my life: the Holy Roman Church. Were I to be cut loose, what would become of me? I would be set adrift upon a vast and boundless ocean and who would anchor me?

I am working in the garden one day, digging out weeds, my mind roiling about the situation I am in, when I pause from my work and look down at my clothes. Prickly burrs from the weeds cling to my skirts. I pick at them, quietly mulling over a passage of Scripture I have read the previous day.

It is a single verse, from the fifteenth chapter of St John, where our Lord speaks of the vine and its branches. In verse five He says, "I am the vine, ye are the branches: he that abideth in me, and I in him, the same bringeth forth much fruit: for without me ye can do nothing." I consider this verse, quietly breaking it apart in my mind, just as I have been breaking up the rich clods of earth at my feet.

I think of the burrs that are even now clinging to my skirts, and I think of a branch and how it clings to the vine, drawing nourishment and strength from it. A branch is nothing without the vine, for the vine is its source of life. And then, quietly, like dawn gently stealing over the sleeping earth, the truth settles over me. I see the choice before me as it really is. I had thought that I was struggling to accept Brother Martin's words and the inherent dangers of such a choice, but the truth is that I am struggling to accept the words of Christ.

Yes, the path that Brother Martin is carving before us is fraught with danger and sacrifice. It will cost me something to embrace these new teachings. I will have to leave the safety of the convent and face a world that is hostile and alien, not only to my beliefs but also to my gender. I will have to learn to live in the outside world. I realise that to accept these new teachings will be to relinquish safety and security. The surety of a roof over my head, food in my belly, a respectable station in life. For if I were to leave this convent, I would be nothing more than a homeless, helpless woman, unprotected and vulnerable in a world that has very little use for me apart from being a wife and mother—and I have no experience in such things. I do not know what it means to be a wife or mother, for I have lived among nuns my entire life.

Sighing, I rise to my feet and dust off my skirts, grasping a single burr in my hand. I realise that, like this little burr, I have to choose what I will stick to. Will it be Christ? Or will it be the safety of the convent? For I know that I cannot have both.

Summer, 1522

It is Margaret who finally makes a decision. Or at least takes some action.

There are twelve of us and we have all decided that we cannot turn our backs on the truths we have learned. I have read the book of Romans again and again, and I find that I cannot deny the pure beauty of righteousness by faith. I cannot. That book above all others has taught me that I must stick to Christ as that little burr stuck to me. There is no safer place for me to be, not even within the walls of this convent that has been my home for so long. My only safety is in Christ and I must stick to Him always.

But that leaves us with very few options. We all write to our families, tentatively asking if they will have us back, if we can come home. My father does not even reply and his silence speaks volumes. Most of the other sisters find that their families will not have them either. It is a scandal to harbour a runaway nun, not to mention a danger, especially in the times in which we live. No-one wants to be called a heretic and burned.

It is then that Margaret takes it upon herself to write to Martin Luther.

"But what will you say to him?" Veronika asks, eyes wide in disbelief.

"I shall ask him if he can offer us a solution to our present predicament," Margaret says breezily, though I wonder if she is as self-assured as she appears.

"What kind of solution could he possibly offer us?" Ava shakes her head.

Margaret smiles, "Well, we shall soon find out."

And we do, for Brother Martin writes back to Margaret and they begin to devise a plan.

Wittenberg, The Holy Roman Empire of the German Nation
April 5, 1523

Crammed into a fish barrel in the back of a jostling wagon, I remind myself that this is what I wanted: to leave, to be free. But with the stench of rotten fish filling my nose, I can't help but wonder if there might have been a better way to get us out of the convent. Looking up at the sky above me, I see that it is streaked with the pale pink of dawn. *At least I am warm*, I think.

I am dozing when the wagon stops. I snap awake and sit still listening. I hear footsteps crunching on the gravel and then a creak as someone mounts the wagon bed. A face appears above my barrel, blocking out the sun. I let out a breath when I realise it is Herr Koppe. "We're in Torgau," he says. "Do you want to get out here or go on to Wittenberg?"

"On to Wittenberg," I croak through cracked lips. He nods, then goes to the other barrels and I hear him asking the others the same question: Torgau or Wittenberg? Three of the sisters decide to leave. We stop that night in an abandoned barn beside the road where we roll in the mite-ridden hay and sleep for a few fitful hours. Then just before dawn we are on our way again.

It is late the next day when we reach Wittenberg. The wagon clatters over cobbled streets, and I can hear the noise of the marketplace and people going about their business. When the wagon finally comes to a halt, I hear shouts and footsteps, then a familiar creak before Herr Koppe's face appears above me.

"We are here, Fraulein Katharina," he says.

I grip the top of the barrel and haul myself upright, looking around as the others emerge. My legs nearly buckle beneath me as I stand, and I grip the barrels to steady myself as I make my way towards the back of the wagon.

I see a small group of men, standing just behind the wagon, eyeing me and my sisters curiously. If the smell of fish has assaulted them, they do not show it. I move to step down from the wagon and stumble, nearly falling to the ground, my feet are so numb and cramped. One of the men leaps forward and steadies me with an arm around my waist.

"Are you alright, Fraulein?" he asks me, offering me a friendly smile. "I am Spalatin, Master Secretary to Prince Frederick of Saxony."

"Katharina," I smile back, my legs still trembling. "Katharina von Bora."

The other sisters have gotten themselves out of their own barrels and I make quick introductions.

Another man steps up just then. "Nicolaus von Amsdorf," he says smiling. "I am one of Dr Luther's friends. He sends his apologies that he cannot be here, but he has instructed me to take you to your lodgings and make you comfortable."

We all trail after him, the stench of fish billowing around us like a cloud. The good citizens of Wittenberg pause and whisper to each other as we pass by. We left our nuns' habits behind at Nimbschen and our gowns are plain and stained with filth. Our hair is cropped short, our lips dry, and our faces pale with exhaustion. I later hear that when Spalatin described us to Martin Luther he called us a "wretched sight."

Nicolaus takes us to our lodgings and asks, "Now ladies, what would you like to do first? Some food perhaps?"

We all look at each other and, raising my eyebrows in amusement, I politely request, "A bath, Dr von Amsdorf. How quickly do you think you might be able to arrange for us all to have a bath?"

When Dr Luther comes to see us that evening, we are bathed and smelling less like fish, though I am beginning to wonder if what Elsa said was true—that we could wash for a thousand years and never get rid of the smell. Dr Luther is amiable but a little serious, and he greets us formally. He informs us that he will take financial responsibility for us until we are able to get on our feet, though how we are to do this we do not know.

"A marriage perhaps?" he suggests, and we all look back at him silently. Of course, that is what we must do. But we are nuns who have lived in a cloister for most of our lives, and we have no idea how such things are managed.

"How will we go about it?" Veronika finally asks. "Will we need to go out and arrange marriages for ourselves?"

At this, his lips twitch upwards in a small smile. "I will help you, Fraulein von Zeschau," he says. "I will help you all."

Spring, 1525

I am at my wits' end and can stand it no longer when I call for a meeting with Nicolaus von Amsdorf. I try to keep calm, but I find myself fuming by the time he walks into the room and bows politely.

"Good morning to you, Fraulein Katharina," he says pleasantly, taking a seat across from me. I incline my head politely, but then I find that I am too impatient to wait on ceremony.

"I can't stand it anymore, Nicolaus!" I exclaim, and he looks at me with a startled expression. Clearly, he has had no inkling of my frustrations. But then I see his expression soften and he tips his head. "Are you troubled about young Baumgartner?" he asks quietly.

I feel the colour rise in my cheeks and quick tears spring to my eyes. I want to deny that I feel anything for Hieronymus Baumgartner, but I cannot lie and so instead I sigh miserably and drop my head.

"Did he make any promises?" Nicolaus asks gently. I cannot speak, so I simply nod my head once. "You have not heard from him since?"

I clear my throat and raise my head, tipping my chin in a show of bravado, though I feel like my heart has dropped down to my knees. "He has written to Dr Luther," I say, each word stripped clean of any emotion.

Nicolaus considers me for a moment, before sitting back in his chair. "What does he say?"

"He says that his family does not take kindly to the thought of him marrying a runaway nun." I try to hide the edge of bitterness that creeps into my voice, but I can't.

Nicolaus sighs and shakes his head. "I am sorry, Katie. I know this is hard." His gentle, compassionate tone nearly breaks me, but I force myself to hold my emotions in check.

"I need to be married, Nicolaus," I say stiffly. "I am the only one of us, I mean the only one of the nine nuns who came to Wittenberg, that has not found a suitor. I thought..." my voice trails off for a moment. "I thought Hieronymus really cared about me," I say, daring to meet his eyes.

He is silent, watching me sadly. "I am sorry," he says again, and I look away.

"You know," I pause, wrestling with what I need to say. "You know what it means to be a woman in this world. I can't set up a home on my own. I have no way of earning a decent income, no way of supporting myself. I need a man to care for me and my father will not have me and neither will my brothers." I shrug. "So you see, I am really without any hope."

Nicolaus nods. "But you are working currently. At the Cranach home?" he says.

I have been a boarder in the home of Lucas Cranach, the court painter for the Elector of Saxony, but I cannot live there forever and I tell Nicolaus so. "I need a solution," I say, my voice becoming desperate. "I cannot go on like this. It will soon become a stain on my reputation."

"What about Kaspar?" Nicolaus says finally.

I blink at him. "Kaspar Glatz? The pastor?"

He nods watching my reaction. I shake my head. "No, Nicolaus! He is old enough to be my grandfather. How can you even suggest it?"

He raises his hands in an attempt to calm me down. "I am just going through your options, Katie," he says, trying to placate me. "I know you are in an impossible situation and I thought that Kaspar might present a good prospect. He is a good man and he would be kind to you."

"No!" I exclaim. "No! I cannot consent to you marrying me off to...to such an old man!"

The corners of Nicolaus' mouth tug up in a faint smile. "Do you have any other ideas?" he asks.

I take a deep breath and stare him down. This is my opportunity, the one I have prepared myself for over the past few days. "I think," I say slowly, "that at this point it only makes sense for me to marry either yourself or Dr Luther."

He blinks at me, stunned. For a moment I panic. *What am I thinking, proposing marriage to Nicolaus or Martin Luther himself?*

Suddenly, he jumps out of his chair like a man bitten and I am afraid that he is about to bolt right through the door, but he only paces to the fireplace, his back to me. When he turns, his eyes lock onto mine and he searches my face.

"You're serious?" he finally asks.

I sigh and twist my hands together in my lap. "I would hardly joke about something like this," I say. "Listen, Nicolaus, if I could live on my own I would, but I can't. I am not *allowed* to. I need a male guardian to take charge of me."

He walks back to his chair and sits down, then he puts his elbows on his knees and rakes his hands through his hair, completely forgetting about his cap. It falls to the floor and he picks it up, twisting it nervously between his fingers. He gives a soft laugh. "I can't marry you, Katie." He looks up at me and shakes his head. "You would eat me alive."

At this I cannot help but laugh. "I am not so fearful, Nicolaus," I say, grinning.

He smiles back at me and shakes his head again. "I think you are. And I think the only man who could truly manage to be married to you is Martin. The two of you will butt heads successfully and even each other out."

"So you will talk to him?" I ask, hope surging in my heart.

Nicolaus nods and clamps his hat back onto his head. "Yes," he says, his shoulders slumped in resignation. "Yes, I will talk to him."

June 13, 1525

We are married at Martin's home, the Black Cloister, in a small private ceremony. John Bugehagen, one of Martin's closest friends, marries us.

It is a terrible time to be married. Germany is in the throes of a violent peasant revolt. Peasant revolts are nothing new. But this time they claim to be inspired by the teachings of Martin Luther himself. And it is not only the peasants revolting, but preachers who are reform-minded are revolting as well. They are all waving Martin's books to justify their actions, especially his pamphlet "On Christian Freedom," where he says that all true Christians are freed from following the law. Of course, they have misconstrued his words, but a religious revolution seems a good excuse to mount a social one and so Martin's name has been dragged into the thick of it.

Then there is the constant threat of the Edict of Worms that looms large over us. The emperor himself has ordered Martin's arrest, though admittedly, as long as Martin stays in Saxony he is safe, for Prince Frederick has offered him asylum here. But with the world around us going mad, we are never sure of what to expect, even here in Saxony.

Added to all this, our wedding causes such a storm in Christendom that we are astonished. Everyone has an opinion about it. Erasmus writes to us. King Henry VIII of England writes to us. He says that Martin only wanted reform so he could have an excuse to marry. Someone even says that any offspring we have will be the antichrist. I had not expected so much attention but I take it in my stride.

Despite the uncertainty around us, I make it my first order of business to set the house to rights. Martin has been a bachelor for so long that the house is a pig sty. I sweep into his bedroom one morning and stop short in horror when I see the sheets on his bed. He comes ambling in after me and sees the look on my face.

"What?" he asks, looking around the room. "What is it?"

"When did you last wash your sheets?" I ask, approaching the bed with disgust.

"My sheets?" he cocks his head. "I don't know."

"How can you not know? Look at them!"

He does as I ask and shrugs, "They are adequate."

"*Adequate?*" I gasp. "Martin, they are black with filth! We cannot even wash these. They will have to be thrown out!" I reach over and begin to tug the covers off the bed, wrinkling my nose in distaste.

"Oh now, don't be so hasty," he says, furrowing his brow in concentration. "I think it was... I think it was around the time that..." He begins to mumble to himself and I turn back to the task of ripping the sheets off the bed and dumping them on the floor. "A year," I finally hear him say. I turn to face him and stare at him for a moment.

"A year?" I ask.

"A year since I last had my sheets changed," he clarifies. "Or thereabouts."

My mouth drops open in shock. "*A year?*"

He waves his hand dismissively. "Oh, don't go on about it like that! Why must women take so much offence over a little dirt? They will come clean in the wash. Perhaps you could boil them?" he offers helpfully.

I am too appalled to speak. What kind of man doesn't wash his sheets in a year? "Why have you not washed your sheets for so long?" I finally manage, my hands planted on my hips. "Did you not have a washerwoman before we were married?"

He takes a seat in a chair beside the window and shrugs. "I didn't want her coming into my room too frequently. Besides, I had more pressing matters to attend to."

Muttering under my breath, I gather the soiled sheets in my arms before marching out the door.

"You can change them more frequently if you'd like!" he calls out to my retreating back.

Summer, 1526

I settle into my role as the wife of Dr Luther and I begin to enjoy it. We were not in love with each other when we married, but we learn to live together amicably. There is so much to do around the house that I am always busy.

We have a farm, which I run single-handedly, and I take great satisfaction in my work. As I work around the farm, I wear my hair pulled tightly away from my face, the sleeves of my dress rolled up and my apron sitting snugly around me. I walk through the orchards, testing the ripening fruit myself, breathing in its sweet fragrance, directing the workers as they gather in the harvest. Soon we have some of the finest produce in Wittenberg. Sometimes I drive the wagon down to the cattle market to purchase a few head of cattle, and then when they are brought home I drive them out into the fields myself.

I love the work. I love running a farm and a home. When Martin comes home from the university, we sit by the fire and I tell him all about my day—the cattle, the fields, the harvest. He listens, nodding, then tells me what he has been teaching or studying.

I thrive on it. Thanks to my time in a convent, I am well educated—better educated than most women—and we are able to have long discussions in Latin and Greek, arguing back and forth. He hates to yield a point to me, but I am not one to back down. Sometimes we argue theology late into the night. I am grateful to God for giving me a husband who treats me as an equal in every way, especially intellectually. This matters more to me than anything else.

We always have a house full of people, sometimes 40 or more dining with us or living with us. There is never a quiet moment in the Luther household. In the evenings, our table is crowded for supper: Martin's friends from the university, theology students, boarders. They all sit around the table and have deep arguments. Martin likes to call these sessions "table talk." When the food has been set on the table, I sit with the men, the only woman who has a seat at the table. Many of them are Doctors of Theology: Philip Melanchthon, Justus Jonas, Nicolaus von Amsdorf, John Bugenhagen—and then there is me, Katie Luther, and I am unafraid to take on these doctors and study the Bible with them.

Of course, things invariably go off track when Martin and I are on different sides of an argument. The others are then wisely silent. No-one wants to get caught in the crossfire. One night, when I refuse to back down, Martin growls in exasperation, "You are impossible! You convince me of whatever you please and have complete control of the household as well."

I laugh at his outburst. "Is that why you call me Lord Katie?" I ask teasingly.

His mouth settles into a wry grin at the nickname he often calls me by. He looks at me for a moment, his eyes softening. "Yes," he says.

"You will always be my Lord Katie." Then he grunts and mutters, "Female government never did anyone any good."

Giving him a smug smile, I rise from the table and take my leave for the night. For all his tough exterior, Martin Luther has a big soft heart.

One evening I am seated on a stone bench under an apple tree and he is sitting beside me. My great pregnant belly is sticking out in front of me and my back is aching. We have lapsed into a pleasant silence and Martin is reading a letter he has received. He grunts beside me.

"What is it?" I ask, looking away from a little robin chirping on a branch overhead.

"Spalatin is getting married," he says, folding up the letter.

"Oh, that's nice." I close my eyes and breathe deeply, relishing the subtle fragrance of ripening fruit.

"He wants me to come," he says absently.

My eyes fly open and I turn to stare at him, "To come? For his wedding?"

"Yes." He looks at me and does a double take at my shocked expression. "What's wrong?"

"How can he expect you to travel at a time like this?" I ask. "Doesn't he know that it is dangerous? You are one of the most wanted men in Christendom. The pope would gladly see you dead and so would the emperor, the King of England and the King of France. And what about all the peasant revolts? They have barely simmered down!"

He waves his hand dismissively. "Katie, please, the kings of Christendom have better things to occupy their minds than chasing after an irritable German monk, and the pope is too busy fending off the Venetians and the Turks to bother about me. As for the riots, as you just said, they have all but died down."

"They will kill you," I insist loudly, my voice wobbling.

"I doubt that they will have assassins to waylay me on the road to George Spalatin's wedding," he says in exasperation.

"They might," I say.

He sighs and angles himself so he is facing me. "Katie," he begins, in a tone that he uses when he is trying to stay calm and reason with me. But when he sees my face, he stops short frowning. "What's this? Are you… are you *crying*?"

My cheeks flame in embarrassment and I look down, brushing the tears from my eyes. I never cry. So why am I crying now?

"Katie," he takes my hand and waits for me to look at him. "Why are you crying?"

"Because I don't want you to go!" I exclaim, the tears spilling down my cheeks. I wipe them away angrily. *Foolish George Spalatin!*

"My love," he says softly, "I will be perfectly safe. I have travelled to the Diet of Worms and back without coming to any harm. This is a hundred times safer."

"Not really," I mumble. "People know you now."

"Katie," he says patiently, "people knew me then."

"I couldn't bear it if something happened to you, Martin," I say twisting my hands in my lap.

He looks into my eyes and sighs before pulling me close and tucking my head under his chin. "I won't go," he says softly. "I will write to Spalatin and tell him."

I sniffle. "What will you tell him?" I ask.

I can feel his smile against my temple. "I will tell him that my Lord Katie now uses tears to persuade me and that they are far worse than any other tactic she has ever used before."

I straighten myself and punch him in the shoulder, giving him a mock scowl. But he is grinning playfully, and I cannot resist returning his smile. He frames my face with his hands and says softly, "Ah Katie, I wouldn't trade you, not for France or Venice."

"No," I smile. "Neither the French nor the Venetians would put up with you."

We sit there smiling at each other and just like that, it dawns on me that I have fallen in love.

February, 1546

I have just driven into the courtyard and am stepping down from the wagon when I see him. He is standing in the shadow of the stables handing the reins of his horse to one of our grooms. He turns and I immediately recognise his livery. He is one of Elector John Frederick's men. *What is he doing here?* I think frantically. Martin is away from home. He has gone to Eisleben at the request of the Duke of Mansfield to settle a local dispute there.

I open my mouth to greet him, but then I see the expression on his face and I know the message he has for me without him opening his mouth. The breath seeps from my lungs and I shake my head, "No..."

"Frau Luther," he begins. His voice is hoarse and I see tears in his eyes. I feel my legs give way beneath me and I sink to the ground.

"No!" I say again and I put out my hand to stop him. I do not want to hear the words he is about to say.

"Lady mother!" Our 19-year-old son Hans runs out to me and crouches beside me. "Lady mother, are you unwell?" he asks, grasping my hand. It is only then that he sees the man standing there. I see him swallow hard and then he puts on a brave face. "What news?" he asks.

"Dr Luther..." the messenger stumbles over the words. "Dr Luther is...he is...no more." He looks away then and I can feel my entire body begin to tremble.

"How?" Hans is still crouched beside me, holding my hand, and his voice cracks over the single word. He clears his throat and tries again. "How did...What happened?"

"He was taken ill suddenly. They, that is Dr Melanchthon and Dr Jonas, who were with him, did not know what it was, but he was taken ill suddenly and then died in the early hours before dawn."

"When was this?" Hans asks.

"Three days ago," the messenger replies.

Justus Jonas wrote to the elector to inform him of Martin's death, though why he did not write to me first I will never know. I know that there are arrangements to be made and people to speak to but for now I can think of none of that. For now, I need a moment alone. I turn to Hans and lean on his arm.

"Help me up," I say, and he immediately complies. I turn to the messenger and thank him for bringing us the news, then I nod towards the kitchens. "See to your refreshments and I will have a message for you to take back to the elector." The man nods and strides off.

"Come inside, Mama," Hans says gently and tugs on my arm, but I don't want to go inside. I don't want to face the empty chairs and rooms. Martin is not coming home.

I shake my head. "No, Hans. I need to be alone," I say. I walk down towards the apple orchard, my heart beating a war cry. The tears only come when I am seated on our bench, looking at our apple tree, standing cold and forlorn against a grey winter sky. I put my face in my hands, giving way to the sobs, and surrounded by a million memories, I allow myself to grieve for my husband.

They put his body in a coffin and display it in Eisleben, where Justus Jonas preaches a short sermon. *This is fitting*, I think, *for Martin was born there and now he has died there.*

Then they bring his body home to Wittenberg, where he is laid to rest under the pulpit of the Castle Church. He nailed his 95 theses to the doors of this church so long ago. *This too is fitting*, I think. *For where he began his work for the cause of reform, he is laid to rest.*

They come from everywhere to pay their final respects to Dr Luther, the hero of the Reformation, the great champion of righteousness by faith. And yes, he is those things, but he was also my husband, my closest friend, my dearest companion, the man I slowly grew to love deeply and devotedly.

As I watch them lay my husband to rest in the cold vault beneath the pulpit, tears stream down my cheeks. He is gone. He is in every familiar place and object and yet he is not here. He is never coming back.

Before Martin died, he once ominously prophesied, "After my passing, dangerous times will come." He is right. Not three months after he dies, the Imperial army marches through the gates of Wittenberg and Emperor Charles V himself rides up the street to the Castle Church. We all hold our breaths when some of the more staunch Romanists in his train demand that the emperor exhume Martin's body and publicly burn it in the streets, but he does not do this and I am weak with relief and gratitude. Of course, the emperor does not make this decision because he cares for Martin. He is in the midst of a war against the Schmalkaldic League, a group of Protestant German princes who have defied his authority. Though it seems the princes are losing, the emperor does not want to stir up undue strife by publicly desecrating the body of Martin Luther.

The entrance of the Imperial army forces us to abandon our beloved home in Wittenberg. Not only do I lose Martin, but I also lose the home that we shared together. I am numb with grief.

When we return to Wittenberg a year later, we find that all our property has been confiscated. All that is left is our home and even that has been ravaged by war. I beg for money, for help, and rebuild our home to operate as a boarding house, hoping to make some money from that but times are hard. All I have to lean on is the sure arm of God and He does not forsake me. Everything that Martin and I have spoken of, all our theological disputes and our Bible study now converge on this single point.

The truth that was so long in my head now filters into my heart and I learn to live by faith. I learn what it means to lean on God. They are difficult years but in many ways they are precious years, for they teach me lessons that I would not otherwise have learned. I know, as I struggle through year after year as a widow with children, that Christ is indeed a father to the fatherless and a husband to widows. He is my refuge and I cling to Him in the darkest hour of my need.

September, 1552

The plague sweeps through Wittenberg. Bodies pile in street corners and my boarders disappear. The students leave next. Everyone is leaving, running away from the Black Death that sweeps over us. I decide that I must leave too. The children are all grown now but they are still with me, and I send them ahead to Torgau. I load our last belongings into the wagon and then climb onto the seat. Gathering up the reins, I take one last look at our beloved home. I feel that it is finally time to say goodbye and a little ache forms in my heart. It is like saying goodbye to Martin all over again.

The road to Torgau is thronged with people, a mass of humanity all moving in the same direction and my progress is slow. I have just come to an open country lane when something frightens the horses and they rear back. "Whoa," I call pulling on the reins, but they break into a gallop.

The wagon rattles and bounces as I struggle to bring the animals under control, but I cannot. *It's going to overturn*, I think desperately. Finally, I make a split-second decision and heave myself out of the wagon. I bounce and roll, coming to a stop in a cold puddle of water. Moaning, I roll over and shut my eyes.

"Frau Luther," I hear someone gasp. They place me on the back of a wagon and I am jostled down the road to Torgau, intense pain shooting through me at each bump.

Three months later, I know that I do not have long to live. I have lived a full life. A life that not many women have had the privilege of living, but as I breathe my last breaths only one thing seems to matter to me. I open my mouth to speak but no sound comes out.

"What is it, Mama?" Hans asks, coming near to me and clasping my cold hand in his.

I try again, my voice nothing more than a whisper. "I . . . I will stick to Christ," I say haltingly, "as a . . . burr to a . . . cloth."

I lie back with the effort and close my eyes. *I will stick to Christ*, I say to myself, as a delicious drowsiness overtakes me. *I will stick to Christ*, I think as I drift off to sleep.

Katharina von Bora (1499–1552) is often referred to as the First Lady of the Reformation. Her marriage to Martin Luther caused a firestorm in Christendom but was an important development in the Reformation. The Luthers' marriage became a role model for what a Protestant home and a married clergyman's home could look like. The courage and resilience Katharina showed in embracing the teachings of Martin Luther and escaping from the convent that had been her home since early childhood also demonstrated itself in the way she raised her children, ran the family farm and supported her husband's work in ministry, setting the tone for family life within the new reform movement.

2

Olympia Morata
IN THE MIDST OF PURE LIGHT

Schweinfurt, The Holy Roman Empire of The German Nation

January, 1554

I am teaching my brother Latin in the library when a window suddenly shatters, raining splinters of glass into the room. Immediately, we dive to the floor. *They are mad*, I think, as we huddle together behind the table we were seated at. *They are mad to attack us in the middle of the day like this.*

"Are they going to come through the window?" Emilio whispers, trying to look.

"Hush!" I tell him, pushing his head against the floor and gingerly raising mine. The window on the far side of the room is framed with jagged shards of glass and a rock lies on the wooden floor beneath. Through it, I hear shouts and screams, but they don't sound like they are approaching. "I think it was a passing rock," I say cautiously, not moving yet.

"*Olympia!*" Emilio whines, and I realise that my hand is still on the back of his head, pressing his face uncomfortably against the floor.

"Sorry," I murmur, releasing him. The voices outside the window are fading into the distance now and I decide that it is safe to stand.

"We should get Andrew," Emilio says, and I nod.

"Come on," I say, grabbing Emilio's hand and rushing him towards the door.

We quickly make our way out of the library and shut the door behind us. We have been trying to regain some semblance of normalcy this morning by returning to our studies, but it is not to be. The rock, thrown heedlessly through our window, is a grim reminder of the circumstances in which we live.

The siege of Schweinfurt has been limping along for almost nine months now and food and resources are becoming increasingly scarce. The siege is the result of a war between a handful of German princes and Prince Albert of Brandenburg. The war doesn't have anything to do with the people of Schweinfurt at all. Or it didn't until Prince Albert and his army seized Schweinfurt and took cover here. When they heard of his plan, the German princes surrounded the city and besieged it in an attempt to force Prince Albert out of hiding. We do not know which is worse, the armies outside the walls or the army of Prince Albert of Brandenburg within.

"Olympia?" Andrew strides down the hallway towards us, his gentle eyes narrowed on me, assessing if I am hurt or not.

"Oh Andrew!" I cling to him and take a moment to steady myself.

"What happened?" he asks, easing himself away from me and searching my face.

"Someone threw a rock through the window," Emilio offers helpfully.

"What? Are you alright?" My husband's gaze darts between my brother and myself, and we both nod.

"We were sitting at the table away from the window," I say. "It just shattered the glass and..."

A loud crash makes us all jump. Andrew releases me and runs down the short hallway towards the front parlour, where he keeps his long sword. Emilio and I turn to follow. But then we hear the loud splintering of wood, followed by shouts and the heavy tramp of boots inside the house. I gasp and pull Emilio to my side. I turn him around and run back towards the library, away from the noise.

The siege has made the army of Prince Albert desperate. They are already mercenaries, fighting for pay, but the lack of food and funds has turned them savage and they regularly loot and plunder homes in the city. So far we have been safe, but it looks like our time has come.

I pull the door of the library open and hurry Emilio inside with me, shutting the door behind us.

"Quick," I tell him. "Help me grab the table and move it against the door."

Together we manage to drag the heavy table across the room and push it against the door, then we take shelter in a corner behind a bookcase and wait. We hear crashes and shouts and the occasional word of profanity as soldiers move through the house. Silently, I pray for Andrew, hoping that he has had the good sense to conceal himself and not try to face these brutes alone.

He is a doctor and his little apothecary room is filled with vials and powders and cures. I pray that they spare that at least, for he needs it all. Medication is in short supply in the town and many have taken ill because of the terrible living conditions we have all been subjected to. Andrew goes out daily, caring for the sick and helping any way he can.

A crash against the door of the library makes us both jump.

"Someone is trying to get in!" Emilio whispers and I nod, motioning for him to be quiet. I squeeze my eyes shut and begin to pray, pleading with God to keep us safe.

After a while, the soldier at the door gives up his grunting and shoving and we hear his footsteps move back down the hallway. I allow myself a tiny sigh of relief and thank God for his mercy, then I clutch Emilio closer and let my mind wander. Anything to distract me from the horror of our present reality.

I close my eyes and think of home. I think of the palace of Duke Ercole of Ferrara, where I grew up as the companion and friend of Princess Anna. I can still smell the savoury pastries and the marzipan sweets that we would sneak into our rooms from the kitchens at night. Food—so much food. And good clothes. Yards of silk and velvet and brocade in every colour imaginable, sewn into the latest fashions, and soft leather shoes. The masques and dances, the revelry of an intelligent, cultured Italian court. And most of all, the books. All the books a girl could want. The best books Italy has to offer.

I think of Papa. My intelligent Papa, who was one of the leading professors at the University of Ferrara. His name, Fulvio Morato, was known throughout Italy at the height of the Renaissance. It didn't matter to him that I was a girl. He valued my mind, placing me on an equal footing with the men he taught at the university. He tutored me at home and no effort was spared to ensure that I had the best education from the best scholars in Italy.

By the time I was fourteen, I was lecturing publicly in Latin, had written a defence of the Roman philosopher Cicero and was known for my proficiency in Greek, particularly the poetry of Homer. It was these accomplishments that caught the attention of the Duke and Duchess of Ferrara. Duchess Renee brought me to the palace to be a companion to her daughter Anna, a sparring partner who would challenge her mind to grow. I introduced Anna to the joys of Aristotle, Ovid and Euclid. We studied and debated everything from philosophy to geography and politics. It was unconventional for a girl to be so educated, but I thrived on the academic opportunities my father's station in life and my association with the ducal court provided for me.

I lived at court for nine years and while I was there Duchess Renee introduced me to the Scriptures. She had learned the reformed faith from her mentor Queen Margaret of Navarre at the French court. So while we explored Aristotle's *Nicomachean Ethics* and devoured Homer's *Odyssey*, we also plumbed the depths of the Bible. More than anything else I ever read, it was the Bible that changed me, irrevocably, completely. I even began to lecture on the works of John Calvin and the new reformist ideas that were taking root all around us.

The new teachings opened my eyes so that I could no longer accept what I had known as a child. It was like walking through an open doorway into a chamber filled with light and only then realising that you had lived in darkness all your life. It was like coming to dwell in the midst of pure light.

But then Papa fell ill and I left court to be with him and care for my younger sisters and brother. After Papa died, I was not allowed to return to court. I **didn't** know why, and I was heartbroken. But it was during this time that I met Andrew Grunthler, a handsome young medical student. We met at the home of our beloved friend and mentor John Sciapi and we fell in love over intellectual debates and a shared love for the cross of Christ. When Andrew asked me to marry him and leave Ferrara to live in his native Germany, there was only one answer I could give him: yes, a thousand times over.

We left Italy and I brought my brother Emilio with us. Emilio is the youngest, the baby and the only boy, and I hoped to relieve Mama of some of the stress that had fallen upon her after Papa died. And now, here we are. In the middle of a siege, clinging to our lives by a thread, and Emilio a hundred times more vulnerable than he would have been at home in Italy. I squeeze him a bit tighter at the thought.

"I think they have gone," Emilio whispers, pulling away from my stranglehold and trying to stand.

"Stop!" I tell him fiercely. "You do not know that."

"You stop, Olympia!" he snaps, prying himself loose and struggling to his feet.

"*Emilio Fulvio Morato!*" I hiss, in my fiercest big sister voice. "Come back here this instant!"

"Stop smothering me, Olympia!" he shoots back. "I'm a man! I ought to be out there helping Andrew defend our home and our women."

"Your women?" I say, raising an eyebrow. "*You* have no *women*, and for your information you are not a man—you're barely a youth."

"I'm twelve years old," he replies, drawing his scrawny frame up to his full height. "And fully able to defend myself should the need arise. I don't need my sister coddling me!" With that, he starts pulling the table away from the door.

"What are you doing?" I ask him, scrambling to my feet to stop him. "For all we know, those marauding fools are still out there tearing our home apart piece by piece. If they were to lay their hands on you, there is no telling what they would do to you. What would I tell Mama? That her only son is dead because he was too much of a fool to take cover when he should have?"

"You can tell her I died with honour while defending my sister," he grunts, continuing to push against the table.

"Emilio!" I am sixteen years older than him and yet my commanding tone has no effect on him whatsoever. He simply glares at me and continues his futile efforts.

I am ready to drag him away from the table by force, when we hear Andrew's voice at the door. "Olympia? Emilio?"

"We're here!" I cry out, jumping to help Emilio. The table seems to have gained weight and we struggle to move it.

"What have you put against the door?" Andrew asks.

"The study table," I grunt, pushing and tugging. Andrew begins to push and between the three of us we manage to get the door open. "Are they gone?" I ask, brushing back the strands of hair that have come loose around my face. Andrew nods, regarding me across the table. "How bad is the damage?" I ask. I am afraid to hear what he has to say. Andrew has taken up a position here in Schweinfurt at the request of the city authorities and though we make a comfortable living and keep a well-staffed home, we are far from wealthy.

"It isn't too bad," he says quietly. "They did not do much damage. They only took what valuables they could gather and all the food they could get their hands on."

I do not know how to react. When I hear about the food, I want to cry. Food is in such short supply in the city that every morsel counts. We have meagre stores and a household to feed.

But then I think of the fact that they have not touched a single one of my books or my papers and am content that I shall live. I have been working on translations of the Psalms into Greek hexameters and sapphics which Andrew has set to music. It is some of our finest work and I am relieved that all the manuscripts are safe.

Andrew edges around the table and comes to stand by me. "Do you think..." he begins, then seems to struggle to put his thoughts into words.

34

I look up into his eyes, trying to work out what he wants to say. *Linz*, I think. *He is wondering what our lives would be like if he had accepted the position he was offered in Linz.*

"Do you wish we had gone to Linz?" I whisper, and he sighs.

He wanders towards the broken window, his boots crunching over the shards of glass scattered on the floor. He turns to face me. "We would have been safe," he says.

"But at what cost, Andrew?" I ask, careful to keep censure out of my voice. I pick my way over to him and lay a gentle hand on his shoulder. "I know the position was lucrative, but you know what they were expecting."

Andrew nods. "Yes. They were expecting us to give up our reformed faith in exchange for the position. I could not...*we* could not sell our faith so cheaply. But there are times I wish we were anywhere besides here. At least if we were in Linz, we'd be in trouble for a worthy cause—standing for our faith. Here we are just victims caught in the crossfire of a passel of princes fighting a petty war." He waves at the broken window.

"We should have just gone home," Emilio pipes up from behind me.

I turn to him and smile. "Do you miss Ferrara?" I ask him.

He shrugs and looks away. "I miss having a full belly at night," he mumbles.

I walk over to him and put my hands on his shoulders. "You know why we can't go back, don't you, Emilio?" For a moment he just stares at me, but then he nods. We both know why we can never go back home. Already, so many have been burned for embracing the new teachings. The Romanists have kindled the fires and raised the Inquisition, determined to stamp out the heresy they say is growing like a weed in their own backyard.

We are in Schweinfurt because we cannot go back and we cannot go forward. Not unless we sacrifice our faith and that is something we are not willing to do. We cannot sacrifice the truths we hold dear—not for all the prestigious university positions in Europe, not for the familiar comforts of home. When we left Ferrara, we were not exiles, but now we might as well be. And yet even here, in the heartland of reformist thought, we are not safe. We have avoided religious persecution—for though the majority of those who live in Bavaria are Catholics, Schweinfurt has been a reformist city for the last thirteen years—but instead, we are in the middle of a war. It is as though God would teach us that our safety is not found in our location but in Him alone. If this is the lesson He means to teach me, then it is a lesson I mean to learn.

With the help of our servants, Emilio and I set the house to rights. The broken windows are boarded up, the broken front door is patched and rehung on its hinges. We scour the larder and cellar, taking stock of what supplies we have left. The scullery maid comes to say that the markets are empty.

In the midst of all this, Andrew slips out to tend to patients. We wait and wait for him to come home, but eventually we have some thin broth and I send Emilio to bed. When Andrew finally returns, he is pale and shaking. I go to him, a short tallow taper in my hand. When I kiss his cheek, I gasp. "You are burning with fever," I say, and he nods.

"I haven't been feeling well since morning," he says raspily.

"Why didn't you say anything?" I ask him, leading him to our room and helping him change and get into bed. He closes his eyes and I brush my fingers across his fevered brow.

"Too much happening," he mumbles, weariness lacing his voice. "There's an epidemic," he says suddenly, speaking into the silence. My hand stills on his brow and I look down at his glassy eyes.

"An epidemic?" I say, and he gives a feeble nod of his head.

"It is the new soldiers. Prince Albert has managed to sneak in reinforcements and they have brought some sort of plague with them. They are sick and are spreading it across the city."

"When did it start?" I ask.

"A few weeks ago," he says, his eyes fluttering closed again. "But this week there are cases everywhere."

"Oh Andrew, why didn't you say anything?" I ask. "Have you been caring for those struck by this epidemic all this time?"

He sighs. "What else could I do, Olympia? I am a physician. When people are in distress it is my duty to help."

I look down at his flushed face and feel the sting of tears behind my eyes. I stay up with him all night, sponging his brow with cool cloths, but the fever only worsens. All I can do is watch and pray for God to intervene and save his life. I go down on my knees beside our bed, while my husband sleeps fitfully, the fever burning through him like a ravaging fire.

Oh God! I cry, my heart squeezing painfully. I am tempted to remind God of all the sacrifices we have made. To tell God that we could be living in Linz or Ferrara right now, safe and amply provided for had we not chosen the reformed faith, had we not chosen to believe in salvation by faith in Christ alone, had we not chosen to turn our backs on the church and the mass and the saints, had we not chosen to champion the reading of the Bible in our native language. To tell God that we came to Schweinfurt not because it offered the best position but because we wanted to worship Him freely. To tell God that we deserve a better response to our sacrifices than being besieged on one hand and at the mercy of looting brigands on the other. To tell God that Andrew deserves to be healed.

But this is not what I pour out to God, for I cannot reproach Him. I know that if I had to choose again, I would choose the same path. The truths I have embraced have set me free and I could never turn my back on any of them. To live in the midst of pure light is an incomparable blessing. I will not pray as though God is indebted to me for He is not. It is I am who am indebted to Him.

So instead I choose to recite a psalm as my prayer, Psalm 46, which I have recently translated and which speaks to the depths of my soul: "God is our refuge and strength, a very present help in trouble. Therefore will not we fear, though the earth be removed, and though the mountains be carried into the midst of the sea."

Immediately these words bring me comfort. I continue to speak the psalm, claiming each verse as a promise, a treasure. "He maketh wars to cease unto the end of the earth; he breaketh the bow, and cutteth the spear in sunder; he burneth the chariot in the fire. Be still, and know that I am God."

As I say these words, I remember that the war in which we are caught is in His hand. *Be still, Olympia*, I tell myself, as Andrew's soft, fevered moans reach my ears. *Be still and know that He is God.*

I repeat the last verse of the psalm and cling to the promise it holds, like a shipwrecked man clinging to a shaft of wood in the midst of a raging storm: "The Lord of hosts is with us; the God of Jacob is our refuge." I rise to my feet and go to Andrew. I sponge his forehead again with a cool cloth, knowing that only God's intervention will save my husband.

"The Lord of hosts is with us; the God of Jacob is our refuge," I murmur.

For days I sit beside Andrew, praying and watching and waiting. Now and then, Emilio comes up to relieve me, insisting that I rest while he keeps watch. Sometimes I am amused at his determination to be counted as a man, and at other times I am grateful and fall exhausted into bed. Night after night, we hear cannon fire in the distance. It is at night that the armies battle against each other most fiercely.

We are fortunate that our home is away from the city walls but that doesn't necessarily remove all danger. When I go to the window, I see fires blazing in the distance and the silhouettes of men running to and fro, trying to put out the blaze before it spreads too far.

I think about our conversation a few days earlier, about whether we did the right thing in coming to Germany. There has been so much unrest here since the death of Martin Luther, so much fighting. *And yet where else could we have gone?* I think. *England has a Romanist Queen, France hates reformists, Italy is ready to flay them alive, Spain is the most Romanist nation in Europe and the Low Countries are riven with strife.*

I move away from the window and settle beside Andrew once more. Switzerland would have been our only other option. I met John Calvin once, when he was visiting the court of the Duchess Renee. But I know in my heart that Andrew would never have been happy with that arrangement. His heart is here, in his homeland. Once again, my mind reaches for the Bible verse that has given me strength and courage over the last few days: "The Lord of hosts is with us; the God of Jacob is our refuge." That is my only hope—to find refuge in God and trust Him for deliverance.

God is merciful to us and hears our prayers. Andrew's fever breaks and soon he is able to sit up and sip a few mouthfuls of weak broth. We have managed to find provisions once more, largely thanks to the means we have at our disposal. Food costs a fortune, but we are able to afford it. I am so grateful to God for this provision, for without adequate nourishment I know that Andrew will not fully recover from his illness.

"Well, at least we have good cheese now," Emilio says, biting into a large hunk with gusto. He closes his eyes and savours the mouthful, chewing slowly before swallowing. I eye him with a wry smile.

"One would think that you had never seen cheese before," I observe.

"I thought I would never see cheese again!" he retorts, taking another bite.

I roll my eyes at his dramatic pronouncement. "You had food in your belly and a roof over your head these past nine months," I tell him, my voice taking on the motherly tone he despises so much. "Which is a lot more than most have had in this city."

It is his turn to roll his eyes at me. "You can save your lecture, Olympia," he says cheekily. "I'm just expressing my gratitude for a morsel of cheese."

Shaking my head and biting back a smile, I walk towards the stairs, balancing the tray with Andrew's food in my hands. I find him sitting up in bed when I enter our bedroom, and he shoots me a wan smile. "I must say, I prefer being a doctor to being a patient," he says.

I smile as I lay the food down on a table and busy myself uncovering the dishes. "I don't think you're ready to begin doctoring again any time soon," I tell him, approaching him with his customary broth.

"Ah, bread today," he says, his eyes lighting up when he sees the thick slices beside the bowl of soup. "And not a moment too soon. That broth is not doing me any good."

"Then you must be getting better," I tell him with a smile. I lay the tray of food on his lap and he begins to eat like a starving man. As he eats, we talk and laugh softly, forgetting our circumstances in gratitude for still having each other. He looks like himself again for the first time since his fever broke.

As I am carrying Andrew's empty dishes downstairs, a loud blast shakes the house. Grabbing my skirts in one hand, I run down the stairs to the kitchen. I am almost there when there is a second blast, louder and closer this time.

"Oh Frau Grunthler! Frau Grunthler!" the scullery maid cries when I reach the kitchen, her eyes wide and her hands twisting the skirt of her apron.

"What is it?" I ask. "What is happening?"

"I can see fire, madam," she replies, gesturing towards the window, just as another loud blast rends the air.

I rush to the window to look. Fire is not an unusual occurrence. We are used to being cannonaded at night and used to the resulting fires. But what I see from the window makes me stop short and gasp. The fire is raging nearby, the inferno rushing from building to building. It is so fierce that I fear it might engulf the entire city.

Another cannon blast shakes the house and Emilio comes running into the kitchen. "Olympia! They are going to blast us into oblivion," he gasps, clutching my arm. "I don't want to die in Schweinfurt, Olympia. I want to see Mama and Vittoria again."

I look down at him and my heart squeezes painfully at the terror I see in his eyes. He may want to be reckoned as a man, but he is still a little boy at heart. I gently squeeze his hand.

"Come" I say, trying to keep my voice modulated and calm. "I need your help." I see a flash of resolve in his eyes and he straightens his shoulders. "I need you to go upstairs and bring Andrew down. We need to take refuge in the cellar." The roar of the cannons seems to be almost unbroken around us now. I gently push him towards the stairs. "Hurry," I urge, and he is off like a shot, running up the stairs and calling Andrew's name.

With the help of the scullery maid, I gather blankets, tapers, matches and food. We make our way down into the cellar and have just begun to make a little pallet for Andrew when he and Emilio come down the steps. Andrew is still weak and needs help walking. I rush over to help relieve some of the burden from Emilio.

We spend the entire night in the cellar and not one of us gets a wink of sleep. The loud booms of the cannons go on all night, making the foundations of the house groan and shudder. We pray, almost unceasingly, pleading with God for deliverance—from the cannons, from the raging fire, from this war.

When morning comes, the guns fall silent. I venture out of the cellar, leaving Andrew and Emilio behind. I take one look out of the window and my hand flies to my mouth. The city is in ruins. Charred and blackened houses are crouched like defeated sentries, their heads bowed, their roofs pulled low over their ears like caps. The garden wall surrounding our own home has been battered. Large chunks of brick lie in ruined heaps, the gaping holes they have left behind charred and blackened. Our house has been spared. *But for how long?* I wonder.

As I stare at the horrors before me, my heart begins to race in my chest. While further afield, reformists are perishing in the flames for their faith, we are threatened by flames for no other reason than being in the wrong place at the wrong time. We came here because we were determined to settle in a place where we could practise our reformist faith freely, but it seems as if that decision has led us into the fiery furnace.

And yet, I tell myself, *the Son of God was with Daniel's friends in the midst of the fiery furnace.* This thought gives me hope. Though we can't see Him or fathom His hand in any of the chaos around us, He is still our refuge, He will not fail us.

June, 1554

We have now been besieged for fourteen interminable months. Summer is upon us, bringing with it a measure of relief from the epidemic that has swept through the city, but still there seems to be no relief from the horrors of war. Nightly, the cannons thunder, igniting new fires, and we sleep in the cellar. It is a wonder that there are any buildings left standing. And yet, Prince Albert and his army do not relent. They simply dig themselves deeper behind the walls of the city and refuse to surrender.

During the day, Andrew goes out to tend to the sick. There are many wounded during the nightly cannon raids but, by the grace of God, not many die. Emilio and I shut ourselves in the library and we continue with his lessons. Being among books calms me and I hope that the mundane routine of school will give us both a sense of normalcy.

But it does not and we are on the very brink of losing our sanity, when one night Prince Albert decides that it is time to give up and go home. The deafening silence awakens Andrew. We have grown so accustomed to sleeping through cannon fire that the stillness is like an alarm. Curious, Andrew crawls out of the cellar to investigate the silence.

"They are withdrawing," he says, his face appearing above us in the open cellar door.

"Withdrawing?" I ask. "Surrendering?"

Emilio runs to the cellar steps and bounds up them in a flash. "I want to watch!"

"Emilio!" I say, scrambling after him. "Don't be daft! We are not going to stand at a window and watch Prince Albert's troops withdrawing, *if* they are even doing so to begin with. It's far too dangerous and..."

"Stop smothering me, Olympia!" he complains, standing beside Andrew and puffing out his chest. "I'm a man and men like to be part of the action."

I glare up at him and Andrew grins, "It's fine," he says to me soothingly. "They really are withdrawing. Quietly too, I might add."

We go to a window in the main parlour and watch as Prince Albert's troops slither out of the city like phantoms or thieves.

"I don't think they are surrendering," I whisper, clutching Andrew's arm. "I think they are trying to evacuate without being detected."

"That's impossible," he murmurs beside me. "The allied army would have sentries guarding every gate of the city."

We stand at the window and watch the quiet flow of soldiers limping by until we are exhausted and ready to sleep. We go back to the cellar, because heaven knows what will happen from one minute to the next.

By the next morning, everything is in an uproar. While part of the besieging army has taken off in pursuit of Prince Albert, the rest of the soldiers ravage the city. It is as though we are to blame for allowing Prince Albert and his forces to slip away unnoticed. For, by some miracle, he has done just that. And now they are angry at the people of Schweinfurt completely without cause, for we have been caught in a siege that has nothing to do with us for fourteen miserable months and we are not responsible for Prince Albert's escape now. But as we soon find out, none of this matters.

That day we come to realise that there is nothing quite so frightening as an army lacking restraint. The soldiers sweep through the city, looting, burning and destroying everything in their path.

"We must leave," Andrew says quietly, as we peer out at the mayhem. "It will not be long before they make their way here and then we will not escape with our lives."

"I need to pack," I say, turning towards the library, intent on packing my manuscripts and my most valuable books.

"Olympia," he says seriously, putting his hand on my arm. "Beloved, there is no time. Besides, we cannot carry anything. We must leave with the clothes on our backs."

I stare at him slack-jawed. "I am not leaving my books and manuscripts, Andrew," I say.

He shakes his head. "We have to. They may be making their way towards our home as we speak. If we do not leave now, we will not be able to escape."

I open my mouth to argue but he shakes his head, "Think of Emilio," he says softly. That stops me in my tracks. I would never forgive myself if anything happened to him.

The three of us slip out the back door and move as quickly as we can away from the chaos that is advancing. Others are doing the same and we are like a mass of fleeing animals. "Follow me," Andrew says. He charges ahead of the crowd, looking for a safe route out of the city. I hold Emilio's hand firmly in mine. We stumble over debris and loose cobblestones, but we keep going. We must reach the gates and get out of the city as fast as we can. Once we escape, it will likely take hours of walking to find someone to give us refuge. The siege has desolated the surrounding area.

As we make our way through an alley, we stumble upon a group of soldiers looting a home. Horrified, we come to a halt and Andrew is about to turn us around when they spot us.

"And what do we have here?" one of them asks, his mouth spreading wide in a mocking grin.

"Looks like a couple of fleeing birds," another one sniggers.

Andrew immediately comes to stand in front of Emilio and I. "We mean you no harm," he says, hands up, palms facing outwards in a placating gesture. "I am Dr Andrew Grunthler, and my wife and I are merely seeking to leave the city." The men regard us silently. "We have nothing of value on our persons," Andrew continues, as though he is reading their minds.

"Oh, I beg to differ, good doctor," the first says, eyeing Andrew. "That looks like a mighty fine doublet and hose to me." He laughs and the others join in. "We'll take your clothes," he says, gesturing at us with the knife in his hand. "All three of you."

I begin to tremble and pray. I have heard of the horrors of war and what can happen to women. *Oh God, please*, I beg silently. *Please spare me. Don't let them violate me. Not here. Not in front of my husband and my brother.*

"I would be happy to give you my clothes and boots," Andrews says slowly, "but I ask that you spare my wife and her young brother." He inclines his head towards us as we cower behind him praying.

The man who has the knife in his hand grins. "Oh, we'll spare them alright," he says. "We'll spare them the trouble of walking out of town fully clothed."

There is raucous laughter and one of the men grabs Andrew and hauls him away. Emilio and I are suddenly left without our protector and I instinctively put myself between him and the men, shielding him. "Please," I whisper, but they begin to advance on me.

"*No!*" Andrew cries, and I see him struggling against the man who holds him. "Don't you dare lay a finger on my wife!"

His cries fall on deaf ears. One of them grabs my arm roughly and begins to haul me towards himself. Suddenly, I hear a guttural cry behind me. I whip my head around in time to see Emilio charging towards the man. For an instant, all the men are frozen in shock and then one of them grabs Emilio by his collar and raises him into the air.

But Emilio is not perturbed. His legs kick and flail beneath him and he swings his fists sideways in the hopes of hitting the man. "Don't you lay a finger on my sister!" he yells, twisting and writhing in the man's grasp.

For a single terror-stricken moment I am afraid that they will kill him. But then the man grunts and lowers Emilio to the ground, his hand still tightly gripping the back of his shirt. "Be still!" he commands, but Emilio continues to struggle. "Be still or I will run your sister through with my sword!" He draws the sword that is sheathed at his side.

"Emilio, be still!" Andrew commands, his voice hoarse with fear.

Eyes wide, Emilio ceases his struggles and stares at me, the blood draining from his face. I whimper in fear, my thoughts spinning too wildly to form a coherent prayer. *Oh God!* I cry again and again. *Oh God!* The man holding me jerks me upright, for my knees have begun to buckle.

Then one of the men speaks. His voice is low and commanding. "We will not harm you," he says, his gaze roving over the men who surround us. "We will not lay a hand on the woman. But all of you," he says, "must strip down to your underclothes and give us your clothes, jewellery and shoes." He nods towards Andrew's sturdy, expensive boots.

Silently, tears of gratitude and terror spilling down my cheeks, I strip off my velvet and brocade gown. I take the earrings from my ears and the chain from around my neck and hesitate for the slightest moment before slipping off my rings, one of which Andrew gave me on our wedding day. They bundle up our belongings and leave us there in the street, Andrew and Emilio in their undershirts and hose and me in my shift. But at least we are alive and unharmed—for this we are grateful.

Once they have gone, Emilio slips his hand into mine and I give it a hard squeeze. I smile down at him, fresh tears slipping down my cheeks. "Thank you," I whisper. "Papa would have been so proud of you, and Mama will be so proud when I tell her." He nods, tears shimmering in his own eyes.

We decide that the town of Hammelburg, about nine miles away from Schweinfurt, would be the best place for us to seek refuge and Andrew leads the way. I am exhausted and the hot summer sun beats down on us. The stress of the long siege and the lack of food and sleep has worn me down. The terror of our encounter with the plundering soldiers has been the final straw. We have not gone many miles before the weight of everything that has happened hits me. I sink down onto the warm earth and begin to cry.

"Olympia?" Andrew is by my side in an instant, his hand brushing my damp forehead.

"I cannot, Andrew," I say, gulping through heaving sobs. "I cannot go another step."

"Shhh," he soothes, gathering me close, gently rocking my shaking body. "You can, Olympia," he says quietly, fiercely. "You can because God is your strength and He does not try us more than we are able to bear. You can."

At his words, I remember a scripture that I asked Emilio to commit to memory not long ago. While my shoulders continue to shake with sobs, I repeat the words silently: "That the trial of your faith, being much more precious than of gold that perisheth, though it be tried with fire, might be found unto praise and honour and glory at the appearing of Jesus Christ."

Gradually, my sobbing eases and, as I rest my head on Andrew's shoulder, I realise with a jolt that what we have experienced during the siege has been just this: a trial of our faith. I realise that God's blessings are sometimes not what we make them out to be. Sometimes they come in the guise of trials that we find hard to bear. In the form of cannons, sicknesses and marauding armies. Iron must be placed in the white-hot flames of a foundry before it is malleable enough to be moulded. And it is in the crucible of trials that we become malleable enough for God to mould us. The life we left behind, the affluence we declined, would not have given us the opportunities for growth that we have had over the last fourteen months.

I think of the trials of Job and I raise my head from Andrew's shoulder and look into his eyes. "Though he slay me," I say quietly, "yet will I trust in him." A smile spreads across Andrew's face and he nods. Slowly, he gets to his feet, helps me up and we continue our journey.

Erbach, The Holy Roman Empire of the German Nation Summer, 1554

We eventually find refuge in the home of the Count of Erbach in Hesse. On our first night in their home, his wife, the Countess Elizabeth clucks over me like my own mother would have had she seen me in such a state. My hair is filthy and matted, my shift tattered, and my feet cracked, bleeding and unrecognisable. She immediately orders a bath. They bring the big wooden tub into my room and I watch, standing by the window, as they line it with linen sheets. They pour jug after jug of steaming water into it and then bring in scented soap.

The warm water sends prickles of pain shooting through the cuts and bruises that are spread over my body, but even that cannot quell the sense of unmitigated joy that spreads over me. A maid lathers my hair with the sweet soap, then I shut my eyes and lean back as she pours jugfuls of water over me to rinse the soap out. It is like a slice of heaven.

When I go down for dinner, I am wearing a velvet gown and soft leather shoes. My feet have been rubbed with salve and my hair pinned up beneath a cap. I feel like a new woman and, in many respects, I suppose I am. The siege of Schweinfurt has changed me in ways I never thought possible. That night as I sink into the soft, cool sheets, I whisper a prayer of gratitude to God, thanking Him not only for His provision but also for His faithfulness in the midst of trial.

The next morning, we go to chapel with our hosts. They share our faith, for Hesse is largely a reformist state. I soak in the reading of the Scriptures as the dry ground takes in dew. It has been so long since I have sat and listened to a sermon, so long since we have been able to worship with those of like mind. And then after breakfast they show me their library and I am complete. I tell Andrew and Emilio that they must not expect to see me for the rest of the day, and I sit reading by the light of candles till they burn low and I am forced to go to bed.

We spend the summer in Erbach, and as the days lengthen into weeks, I feel the burden and distress of the months of siege slowly melt away. But it doesn't take much to bring the old fears back. One day, Emilio and I are seated in the library working on his lessons when Andrew bursts in.

"What is it?" I gasp, my eyes going wide. I glance at Emilio and see that he is rigid in his chair, both of us fearing the worst.

"You will not believe it!" Andrew exclaims, and it is only then that I see the excitement on his face and the pounding of my heart eases.

"What?" I repeat, and he grins at me like a schoolboy.

"I have been offered the Chair of Medicine at the University of Heidelberg!" he says.

"What?" I whisper again.

"The Chair of Medicine, my love!" Andrew grabs me around the waist and swings me into the air in excitement.

I clutch his shoulders and look down into his face. "How?" I ask.

He sets me down and shoots Emilio a grin. "You know the Countess Elizabeth is sister to Prince Frederick, the Elector of the Palatinate," he explains, and I nod. "Well, the Count has been corresponding with the Prince about our situation, and Prince Frederick has offered me the Chair of Medicine in Heidelberg, which is within his jurisdiction."

I shake my head in disbelief and launch myself at him, laughing. "Oh, praise God!" I say breathlessly, as he twirls me around the room. "Oh, praise God for hearing our prayers!"

That night when I go into Emilio's room to bid him goodnight, he is more pensive than usual. "What is it?" I ask, smiling down at him and easing the book that he is reading out of his fingers.

He lets it go reluctantly and sits up in bed. "Olympia," he says, and his face is so serious that it sobers me as well.

"Yes," I venture, a nervous flutter in my stomach. I feel as though we are about to have one of our serious philosophical conversations about life, and Emilio's questions are alarmingly astute for a boy his age. I whisper a silent prayer for help and nod encouragingly.

"God works in strange ways, don't you think?" he finally asks.

I tip my head, considering his statement. "Why do you say that?" I reply.

"Well, we were in Schweinfurt because of certain choices that you and Andrew made." He pauses and studies me. "You chose to leave Italy and come to Germany"

"Yes, because Germany is Andrew's home," I say.

Emilio nods, "Yes, but even when things started to go bad and we could have gone back to Italy, you did not want to, because you could exercise your faith more freely here in Germany."

"Yes," I nod "That is true."

He pauses again, as though gathering his thoughts, and then continues, "When Andrew was offered that position in Linz, it would have been easy to take it, but you both chose to decline it, so that you could continue to exercise your faith freely, without fear of threat or coercion."

I nod patiently, waiting for him to get to his point. "Because of those decisions, because you chose faithfulness to God over anything else, we ended up being in Schweinfurt in the midst of a war. Then we had to leave everything behind. Then we were robbed and nearly killed." He lists all the calamities that have befallen us with clinical precision, striking them off his fingers one by one. "It almost seems like being faithful to God brought a plague on us."

"Emilio," I say gently, but he shakes his head.

"It's alright," he says. "I have read the book of Job. I know that God was not the author of those trials." He narrows his eyes. "But do you not think sister, that God has brought us in a complete circle?"

"How so?" I ask, curious to hear his thoughts.

"Well, God has given Andrew a good position in Heidelberg. Perhaps even better than the position he turned down in Linz, because we will be able to exercise our faith freely in Heidelberg."

I smile at him and nod. "God is faithful," I say softly.

"He is," he says, with a nod of his own. "But doesn't it seem like God only gave us this blessing after He had made us fit to receive it?"

"What do you mean?" I ask.

"Well, our trials, they led us to . . . to choose what we value most"

"Yes, trials have a way of doing that. Of stripping us of all pretence and laying bare our bones. And, like you said, that helps us to choose what we value most."

"I know," he says. "And I was thinking that maybe that's why God is sending Andrew to Heidelberg, and you and me as well. Not only to teach medicine and the arts but to help others decide what they value most too."

I smile and nod. "You are very wise, Emilio Fulvio Morato. Wise like Papa." I lean forward and kiss his forehead. "God's ways are not our ways, Emilio. They are higher, but they are also grander and span eternity in a single bound. It is always safest to trust Him."

He lies down in his bed and nods. "Yes," he says, stifling a yawn. "As you are always telling me, it is like dwelling in the midst of pure light."

I smile and smooth the hair on his forehead. "Yes, to trust Him is to dwell in the midst of pure light, always."

Olympia Morata (c. 1526–1555) was an Italian scholar who embraced the reformist thinking during the brief Italian Reformation. She was educated by her father, Fulvio Pellegrino Morato, who was a professor at the University of Ferrara and a tutor at the ducal court. She lectured on the principles of the Reformation while she was in Ferrara and frequently corresponded with reformers like John Calvin and Philip Melanchthon. Olympia was a profound Bible scholar and translated portions of the Scriptures. Though many of her writings were destroyed during the siege of Schweinfurt, she continued to write and teach after her arrival in Heidelberg in August, 1554. Sadly, Olympia became ill not long after the family's arrival in Heidelberg. On her death bed, her husband's final words to her were "Courage, my well beloved; you will soon dwell in the midst of that pure light."

3

Margaret of Navarre
TRUE ALLEGIANCE

Nerac, Navarre
Summer, c. 1529

I hear the rhythmic slap of boots against the flagstones of the gallery just outside my presence chamber—the unmistakable sound of someone running, hard and fast. They draw nearer and soon all activity inside the room ceases. Gerard Roussel, who is standing before us, a Bible open on the lectern beside him stops speaking. I hear the clink of metal against metal as the halberdiers of Navarre, stationed outside the doors, cross their halberds to keep out whoever is approaching.

"Halt! Who goes there?" they call. There is a scuffle, then muffled shouts. I jump to my feet and my ladies gasp around me. Then there is a dull thud and the doors shudder, as though someone has flung themselves against the heavy wood, like a bird against a window. "I bear a message for the queen," someone shouts, and immediately I walk to the doors and fling them open.

The scene that greets me pulls me up short. The halberdiers are clutching a struggling youth who seems undeterred by the menacing halberds hovering over his head.

"Your Highness," he gasps when he sees me, his eyes wild. "A word, your grace."

I instantly recognise him. He is one of the grooms I put to work for me this morning. "Release him," I say, and the halberdiers reluctantly let him go. Once he is inside my presence chamber, I shut the doors behind us and turn on him. "Well?" I ask.

"The king approaches," he gasps.

Those three simple words set us all into motion like players in a well-rehearsed masque. Monsieur Roussel is quietly and quickly ushered out of the room and through a back entrance to a waiting horse. The Bible is tucked away, as is every other visible token of what has been happening in my rooms.

I dismiss the groom with a nod of my head and he bows low before retreating. He looks terrified and I know what he is thinking. I know what they are all thinking. They are thinking that my interest in reformist ideas will bring them all to the burning, but I refuse to accept that. I will not believe that we are so narrow-minded in Navarre that we cannot hear messages from the Bible that might differ from our own long-cherished opinions.

My husband, the king, is a devoted Romanist and I consider myself a daughter of the Roman church too, but I have been opening my heart and mind to reformist teachings for some time now and I want my ladies to have the opportunity to hear these ideas too. It grieves me that so many women have few opportunities for education, especially in spiritual things. I have found that the Bible feeds my soul as nothing else can. How can I not be drawn to a message that tells me that, poor sinner that I am, I need only look to Christ for pardon and it will be given me full and free? A message that tells me that I may come boldly before God's throne of grace with no mediator but Christ? *Surely*, I think, *surely none of this can be heresy?*

But I fear my husband would not agree with me. He is not as tolerant as my brother, the King of France. He is more closed-minded and so I must adapt my ways to his foolishness and skulk around like some brigand on the highway. If I want to hear a reformist sermon, I must smuggle in a preacher, pay the groom to watch for my husband and be ready to whisk the preacher away in the event that my husband happens to come upon us unexpectedly.

Like now. When he is supposed to be out hunting with the court but has suddenly come back early.

My ladies and I are just beginning to settle into our seats and take up our sewing when I hear footsteps once more. I sit up straight and prepare myself, for it sounds like an entire armed band is about to descend on me. *Arrange your face, Margaret*, my mother often tells me. *It is a lady's greatest weapon to learn to arrange her face.* And so I arrange my face into an expression of utmost tranquillity and wait for all hell to break loose around my ears.

"Margaret!" I hear Henry's bark before I see his face. He flings open the doors and strides in, his sharp, hawk-like eyes scanning the room in a single sweep.

"Lord husband," I rise and curtsey low. "Was there an abundance of game or a lack of it? You are back so soon."

He stares at me, his gaze cool and assessing. Henry is a handsome man and ten years younger than me. I fancied myself in love with him when I married him but then our marriage fell apart because of his philandering. Now we have a strained relationship. He cannot afford to put me aside because I am sister to the King of France, and I am a firm believer in the sanctity of the marriage covenant, no matter how turbulent the innards of the relationship may be.

"I heard there was more game to be had here at the palace," he says to me finally, and I bite back a smile. Henry is no fool but then neither am I.

"Oh?" I say, raising an eyebrow. "You had thought to catch something here?"

"Don't be coy with me, Margaret," he spits out. "I heard you were having preaching here, with that man Roussel no less. I thought I had made it clear that I do not want reformists here at my court."

"Surely there can be no harm..."

"Enough!" he silences me. "Where is he?"

"Gone," I reply.

Henry's gaze sweeps the room once more, as though he expects Roussel to leap out from behind an arras and scuttle away like some frightened insect. "I warned you, Margaret," he says, the anger radiating off him in waves. "I told you that I will not countenance any more of this reformist foolishness."

"But my brother allows..." I begin.

"I do not care what your brother allows!" he shouts. Then I know that he has really lost control of himself, for were he in his right mind, he would never breathe a word against my brother so openly.

"What has Roussel been saying, Margaret? More of that nonsense about justification by faith?"

"I have never been challenged before," I say, raising my chin a notch. "I listened to numerous sermons from reformist preachers when I was in France, at the court of my brother the king and he never forbade me."

It is foolish to goad a man like Henry, but I cannot help it. I am Margaret of Angouleme, Duchess of Berry, sister of King Francis I of France, and no man will speak to me as though I am some bungling chambermaid!

"You are not now under the protection of *your brother the king*," Henry spits through clenched teeth. "You are in my house, in my kingdom, and you will do as I say."

"And what do you say, my lord?" I ask, my voice as sweet as honey.

He takes a step towards me and I see the veins in his neck pulsing. I am tempted to take a step back but I force myself to stand still. I will not be cowed.

"You are not to entertain reformist preachers in my house," he grinds out.

His words make me realise that we have reached a crossroads and a tiny alarm sounds in my head, telling me to retreat but I refuse to heed it. Taking a deep composing breath, I say to him, "I cannot comply with your wishes, my lord. I have been free to listen to whoever I please in France and it is my right to be granted that same level of toleration here in this kingdom."

"I will not tolerate reformists in my court, Margaret," he shouts. "I forbid it!"

My spine stiffens at his commanding tone and I raise my chin. "You cannot command me, Henry. I am a princess of France and..."

Like a striking snake, swift, venomous and direct, I see his hand and then I feel it connect painfully across my face. I stagger back and I hear my ladies gasp. Involuntarily, my hand goes up to my face, shielding it. My cheek is hot, and I feel the sting of tears in my eyes. My ladies reach out to steady me, but I pull myself upright. Humiliation washes over me in waves but it is soon overtaken by indignation and rage. I cannot believe that he has struck me.

"You will not insult my authority," he says, but his voice sounds distant and hollow. All I can focus on is the heat in my face and the rage in my gut.

"I will not be beaten into submission, my lord," I say with quiet dignity, though every nerve in my body is screaming at me to leap on him and gouge his eyes out.

Henry's eyes narrow and he stares me down. "We shall see about that," he says, before turning on his heel and walking away.

"Yes," I repeat, watching his retreating back. "We shall see."

I am generally not so combative. Or perhaps that is what I think of myself. Sometimes, no matter how well intentioned we are, our perceptions of ourselves fly wide of the mark. I have sent word to my brother of the confrontation with my husband and now I am standing in my privy chamber, watching the road that winds away from the castle. I am expecting reinforcements.

When I married Henry, I had an inkling of turbulence. He is nothing like my late husband. For one thing, he is smarter. I finger the bruise along my jaw; he is also more violent. But perhaps that is because he wants to control me and I refused to be controlled.

My fascination with the new teachings began with letters to William Briconnet, the Bishop of Meaux. Briconnet had read the Bible and spent time with men like Jacques Lefevre, men who had reformist leanings, men who preached the new ideas from every pulpit they were elevated to. Briconnet embraced the simple realities of salvation by faith. Faith that transcended ritual and embraced the transforming grace of God. Pure and deeply personal. It is these things that drew me. The opportunity they presented to approach God directly, as a poor suppliant seeking mercy and grace and finding it, freely and without any merit.

My eyes fix on a small flicker of movement in the distance. I watch intently as the plume of dust encircling the outriders comes into view and there, just near enough for me to see, is the royal standard fluttering in the breeze. I feel a sense of security float over me like a cloud when I see my brother's arms, the arms of the King of France— the delicate fleur-de-lis resting on a sea of blue.

Francis and I have a unique relationship. When our mother was pregnant with me, she prayed for a boy. She was desperate for a boy because a boy means a change of fortune. A girl can only be disposed of to the highest bidder and even then, a bidder with enough money will only come along if her brother or father is important enough. But a boy. A boy can win his family a kingdom and as it turned out for us, that is just what happened.

But I digress. When my mother was pregnant with me she prayed for a boy and she birthed a girl. There was no celebration at my birth. My father was a poor cousin of the king. Near enough to be in line to the throne but not so near that he should have much money. My mother had to wait two more years for a boy and then, when he finally came, she promptly wrapped her entire life around him, as did I.

From the moment I laid eyes on my baby brother, it was love. We have been inseparable all our lives and our mother is the glue that binds us, especially after our father's death. There is even a joke about us, though I think that when people whisper it behind their hands they are only half joking. The other half of what they feel when they say it is a kind of reverential fear. They call us the trinity, the triumvirate. The three Angoulemes who were poor cousins for so long, then suddenly found themselves on the throne. All thanks to our beloved boy. To a great extent, he has made us what we are.

Francis and I are devoted to each other, so when I wrote to him to say that his brother-in-law, the King of Navarre, had struck me, I knew what to expect. He would not allow this insult to go unpunished. I smirk in satisfaction and withdraw from my window. I look around the room at my ladies and arrange my face into a smile, the very picture of a demure French princess. It is time to engage in battle.

When my brother rides up to the Chateau de Nerac, Henry has just returned from hunting again. Chasing after an innocent creature until he has killed it gives him a thrill. But today Henry is not quick enough, for when he comes to greet the king, I am already there, standing on the steps, flanked by servants, my hood pulled back to reveal my pale face and the deep violet bruise that runs along it.

"*Ma mignonne*, my darling!" My brother is off his horse and at my side in a flash. I smile and he pulls up short, eyeing the damage to my face. Instead of kissing me, he embraces me briefly. When we pull apart, Henry is there, terrified and bowing. Francis turns to him with a predatory smile and says very little.

After dinner and a masque, Francis leans over and whispers to Henry, who then looks at me. I am pale and rigid in my chair, watching the entertainment before me. Then Francis rises and the court rises with him. He motions to me and I follow him and Henry out of the great hall, my ladies trailing behind me. We make our way to the king's rooms, the blaze of wall-mounted sconces lighting our way. We pass through the presence chamber, shed our layers of attendants and find ourselves in the king's privy chamber. Just the three of us. The grooms of the chamber leave us, shutting the door with a soft click and I think I see sweat break out across Henry's face in the candlelight.

Francis turns to Henry and for a moment I think that he will strike him, his expression is so fierce. "Must I declare war?" he asks instead, his tone almost pleasant. Henry swallows. "No. No, my lord. That would be... hasty," he says, tripping over his words.

Francis moves to take a seat in one of Henry's chairs. He runs a finger over the arm and studies my husband.

"You struck my sister," Francis says.

"In a moment of passion, my lord. Misguided passion."

"And what is to prevent such a moment from seizing you again?"

Henry is silent. What can he say to that? We have known him since he was a boy. He and Francis are close friends. He knows what Henry is like.

"When my sister was under my protection, in my court," Francis continues, "she was given the freedom to listen to reformed sermons. In fact, I allowed her to host a stream of reformers there. Marot, Roussel, Calvin," Francis pauses, and Henry foolishly steps in.

"But we are a Catholic court here, my lord," he says.

"And you think my court is not?" Francis is affronted that Henry would even hint otherwise.

"Yes...I mean, no. I mean...I cannot countenance this here at my court. I am a loyal son."

"And you think I am not a loyal son of the church?" Francis raises an eyebrow and lets Henry sit uncomfortably for a moment.

"Sister," he now turns to me. "Why should I not throw down a gauntlet of war against this speck of a kingdom for what he has done?"

I eye my brother and am tempted to smile at his little spectacle, but I rein myself in. "Peace, brother," I say softly. "My lord husband only misunderstood my intentions. I did not wish to challenge his authority. I only wished for him to give me freedom. I believe there is no guile in hearing the Word of God."

"Is this true, my lord?" Francis asks Henry. "Was this unfortunate incident only a foolish misunderstanding?"

Henry is silent, warily eyeing us both. He understands what we have done. We have cornered him and now the hunter has become the hunted. Finally, he sighs and sinks into a nearby chair.

"It will not happen again," he mutters, grabbing his jewelled hat from his head. "She can listen to anyone she likes."

Francis smiles warmly. I nod my head, like the grateful wife that I am, and Henry looks at us miserably.

"Excellent," Francis says, jumping up from his chair and walking leisurely over to Henry. He pauses before him and then raises his arm.

I see Henry flinch and Francis' lips twitch with a hint of smugness. He lays his hand on Henry's shoulder gently and then squeezes it. "If you ever lay a finger on my sister again," he says softly, "I will not give you prior warning. France will ravage you with war and reduce you to ashes." He pauses a beat, letting the message sink in and then he grins, almost boyishly. "And now, if you will excuse me, I will retire to my rooms. Tomorrow, Henry, we must hunt. I hear you have excellent game here." He comes and kisses me on both cheeks. "*Ma mignonne*, we must walk tomorrow. I have much news of the court."

When I am back in my rooms, a single thought swirls around in my mind. What would happen if Francis were to treat me as Henry has? To deny me freedom to listen to reformist teachings, to deny me freedom to shelter reformist preachers? For I have indeed sheltered many of them. I have successfully saved many reformists from the flames or from prison, including John Calvin. Thus far, Francis has listened to my pleadings, though I grant not always. There have been a few who have been sacrificed for their faith but not many.

But what would happen if Francis were to change his views? Oh, I know that he has been tolerant towards reform thus far but only because it has posed no real threat to his sovereignty. But what would happen if he were to feel threatened? As he said, he is a loyal son of the church. What would happen if *he* were to forbid me to worship as I do? Then where would I be? I curl deeper under the covers of my bed, pushing hard against these thoughts. I cannot think of them. I dare not.

Paris, France
Spring, 1533

Henry and I are in Paris for Lent and my brother the king is away in Picardy. I am wearing black as I always do these days. I have lost a baby—a son—and I have also lost my mother, the strongest woman I have ever known and the foundation of our family. These blows have come upon me heavily. My brother and I feel the loss of our mother keenly. For so long it has been just the three of us, battling against powerful forces beyond our control. My mother was always our rudder, always setting our course and keeping us on it by sheer force of will. Now that she is gone, Francis and I must continue along the course she charted together.

While I am here at the Louvre, I command an audience with my chaplain and friend Gerard Roussel. It is he who narrowly escaped being flayed alive by Henry on that long ago day in Nerac, when my husband hit me and my brother flew to my aid. Today Roussel will stand before an audience of five hundred and preach the gospel unfettered at the Louvre. I cannot help but feel a smug sense of satisfaction as I take my place and Henry sits beside me. Gerard preaches with power, laying before us all the beauty of Christ crucified. I pay him rapt attention, my whole heart surging in my chest as I listen to him expounding the Scriptures.

The crowds press in around us and three times we have to move to a larger space. But this single sermon grows beyond anything we have imagined. The people are hungry for more and Gerard begins to preach every day. Soon the crowds number more than a thousand, two thousand, three thousand, until there are five thousand people coming to the palace, in the very heart of Paris, to hear him preach. I had never thought for a moment that Paris would open its gates to reform. She is a city entrenched in the old ways, but it does my heart good to see that I am wrong. I long for the people, both men and women, to have more access to biblical teaching, to be able to read the Bible for themselves. And Paris seems willing to hear, willing to open her heart to reform.

But my joy is short-lived, for though a fraction of the population is hungry for more, not all of Paris is ready to countenance reform. Nor are they willing to tolerate it being preached. It begins at the Sorbonne, the University of Paris, with the ravings of a man who is a prominent Doctor of Theology, Noel Beda.

The Sorbonne has always been the cradle of Catholic thought within the kingdom. But it is also within this cradle that reform has been birthed, for there some of the greatest minds of the church also discovered her weak spots, her vulnerabilities, her errors. Men like Jacques Lefevre, William Farel and John Calvin.

The Sorbonne has been savagely divided, just as Europe itself now quivers on the brink of such a division. Gerard Roussel's sermons seem to widen the chasm even further. Noel Beda sets himself against Gerard and indirectly against me, for Gerard is my chaplain.

Henry and I are cloistered within the palace and I am nervous. With my brother away from Paris, I feel weak and vulnerable. Beda must sense this, must smell blood, for he begins to move swiftly. He applies to the Parliament of Paris, the highest judicial body in the land, to stamp out the heresy emanating from the Louvre. He gathers the support of John du Bellay, Bishop of Paris. He does everything in his power to put an end to what is going on within the walls of the palace.

But they cannot stop me and so they cannot stop Gerard from preaching. I command him to continue and he is more than happy to oblige. So while the world outside rages against us, we continue to preach the gospel from the confines of the palace. I will not be cowed by a single angry monk.

But perhaps I miscalculate how deeply entrenched in the old religion Paris is, how deeply resistant she is to any thought of change. For when Gerard's radical preaching does not stop, the masses of Paris take up Beda's chant and take to the streets. I have not expected demonstrations, but I see them as I watch from my rooms in the palace, long processions of Parisians along the banks of the Seine, bent on extricating their beloved city from the grips of this new teaching. Soon every church in Paris is preaching denunciations against the vile heresy of reform.

I am told, when I inquire about their fervour, that they are afraid. They fear that France will be plunged into the same ruin that Germany has experienced. They fear that rioting peasants drunk on these new teachings will overrun Paris, looting churches as they go. Paris cannot tolerate this. France cannot tolerate it.

Then too there is the fear of death, especially with the plague ravaging us on every hand. The people believe that only the pope and the church stand between us and hellfire and so we must not upset these institutions. Far better for us that the Holy Father thinks on our behalf, speaks to God for us and tells us how to be saved, than for us to think for ourselves. We must not upset the delicate balance that has worked well for our fathers for the past thousand years.

So, with this reasoning behind them, of course the people are afraid. And fear is a contagion. It can spread as far and as fast as any plague and destroy twice as many healthy minds and bodies. When I hear all this, I am alarmed, for who would have thought that these new ideas would breed such fear? I never considered that people would be afraid to think for themselves, that they would rather have another man think for them.

But then the situation escalates. For it is no longer only the ardent Romanists demonstrating with their placards, soon the reformists take to the streets. There is graffiti and poetry flying from one camp to the other. "To the stake! To the stake with this heresy," the Romanists chant, "this vile brew which day and night afflicts us." And then my friend Marot, the reformist poet, rises up and cries, "Into the water! Into the water with these seditious fools! Who, instead of divine words, preach to the people conspiracies and nonsense to inspire contentious debate."

Eloquent though he may be, he does no more than add fuel to an already raging fire. Soon there is finger-pointing and a litany of accusations flying back and forth. Some of the reformists encourage me to call for the Catholic clergy to be expelled, but I cannot agree to that. I do not think that simply tearing down the old ways will make way for people to embrace new ways of thought, to help people grow. The situation finally culminates in the worst smear of all. I am called a seditious heretic and accused of conspiring against my brother and the throne. I think they have all gone mad and Paris teeters on the brink of an open revolt.

We are all saved when Francis comes back to the city and restores order. He is incensed at Beda and strips him of his post and banishes him from Paris. It is a victory once again and I am satisfied. As always, my brother has come to my rescue. He has protected me and restored order.

Paris has been cowed by the arrival of her king, but she will not be beaten. There is a fragile truce on the surface but just beneath it anger seethes like a living beast, straining to be unleashed. I shudder when I think about it, for when this beast is unleashed, where will we all find ourselves? And will the protection of my brother be enough? Will Francis' love for me stretch that far? What if it collides with his loyalty to the church? What then? Can I bear to lose my brother's regard? Can I bear for our bond to be severed in order to retain my reformist views, in order to retain the truths that have changed my life?

When I accepted these teachings, I did not ask myself about the costs but now I wonder about them. The highest price for me would be sacrificing my bond with Francis, and as I read my Bible before I go to bed, I wonder if it is a price I am willing to pay.

October, 1534

When I hear of what has happened, I immediately go to see my brother. I am admitted to his presence chamber and it is full of pale-faced courtiers, whispering in low voices. When they see me, a terrible hush falls over the room. I keep my head high and walk towards my brother. His eyes are cold. I have seen this expression on his face before, but it has never been directed at me. It is then that I realise that I have not been told the half of what has taken place.

I curtsey low and wait until he bids me rise. Then with a swift jerk of his head he motions towards his privy chamber and strides towards it. I follow him and a hushed whisper ripples after us. The gentlemen of his chamber fall over themselves to follow us, but he dismisses them with a curt command. When we are alone, he turns to face me and I see a muscle ticking convulsively in his jaw.

"Have you heard?" he asks finally.

I draw in a breath and measure my words. "I have heard there has been trouble," I say carefully. He cuts me off, barking out a short humourless laugh.

"Did you know, sister, that last night, under cover of darkness, hordes of reformists... *your precious reformists*," he spits the words like venom, "went all through the streets of this kingdom and plastered every available surface with this?" He reaches for a broad sheet of paper that lies crumpled on a nearby stool. He thrusts it into my hand and I take it, smoothing out the wrinkles, willing my trembling hands to be still.

I gasp when I read the words boldly emblazoned across the front of the placard. "True articles on the horrible, great and insufferable abuses of the papal mass," Francis repeats furiously, echoing the words that I am reading as though he has read them a hundred times.

I stare at the placard in shock. They have gone too far. "These . . . these were put up," I ask stupidly, "all over the city?"

"These placards, denouncing the mass in the vilest terms, were stuck onto every door and wall in Paris and elsewhere," Francis says, pacing before me like a caged lion. "Rouen, Blois, Orleans," he waves his hands in the air, his voice rising like the tide. "These reformists had the gall to publicly denounce the mass, plastering these placards even onto the doors of churches." He pauses mid-rant and wheels around to face me. "And then, one fool, one insipid fool, had the nerve to plaster one of these onto the door of my privy chamber while I slept."

I gasp when I hear this. To publish an article such as this for private circulation would signal the swift end of the author's life, for France is so inextricably linked with the Roman Church that she will not tolerate any blatant railings against it. But to publish it so publicly, going so far as to place it even on the king's own door! I cannot believe these reformists would be so foolish. Not only have they endangered their own lives, they have endangered the entire movement.

I lift my eyes to my brother's face and find him watching me. He realises that I have grasped the weight of the situation.

"They will all die," he says quietly.

I suck in a sharp breath. "What do you mean?" I ask.

"I won't tolerate it, Margaret," he says. "I have already issued orders to my lieutenant, Morin. Every single reformist in Paris is to be sought out and burned alive for this."

"Francis! You can't!" I begin. "This was foolish. Foolish and ill-timed, but surely . . . surely it doesn't warrant death." But even as I say it, I know my words are silly. Of course it warrants death.

"It was more than foolish and ill-timed, Margaret. It was seditious and you know it. To threaten the church is to threaten the king. The church gives me my authority. These people are traitors to the king, traitors to France."

I recognise the calm, controlled tone in my brother's voice. Even if I had the presence of mind to put on a calm visage, his gaze would strip it away. He lays bare my bones before him. He knows what I am thinking. He knows he is right. I feel a shiver race up my spine. *Why?* I think. *Why have they done this? Who has done it?* He turns and strides to a window embrasure and I hesitantly join him.

"As we speak, Morin is out in the streets," he says, looking down on the bustle of Paris in autumn. The river is flowing lazily by, the trees gently waving their limbs, shedding their golden leaves onto the rich earth. Parisians are going about their business. But I can also feel a tension that is palpable. Fear is in the air.

"Are people afraid?" I ask.

Francis huffs a laugh. "Reformists plastered placards all over Paris while they slept, Margaret. Of course people are afraid. They are saying that reformists will kill them in their beds while they sleep. They are saying that no-one is safe, nothing is sacred."

I am silent, allowing the words to sink in. I remember Aristotle's words from the *Nicomachean Ethics*: "Anybody can become angry that is easy; but to be angry with the right person, and to the right degree, and at the right time, and for the right purpose, and in the right way, that is not within everybody's power, that is not easy."

The same is true, I think, of how we speak the truth. Clearly, this skill is not within the power of whoever is behind these placards. We can no more win people to the cause of reform by publicly tearing down that which they hold dear than if we burned them alive. The irony is not lost on me. They have caused more harm than good, and I fear this blow will cripple the fledgling movement of reform in France.

I sigh and turn away from the window. "A bloodbath is not the solution, Francis," I say quietly. "I agree, this was foolish, rash." I carefully avoid the word seditious. "They should not have done this. There is a way to preach the new teachings—gently, persuasively, respectfully—and this embraces none of that but, be that as it may, it surely doesn't warrant a massacre."

He is quiet and when he speaks, he is still facing the window. "Morin has with him a reformist, one he has taken by surprise and coerced on pain of death. The man is a messenger, apparently. It is he who summons your little reformists to their secret meetings." I freeze, going completely still as I take in what he is saying. "This little peasant is even now going from door to door and pointing out every single heretic in the city."

"He is betraying his own?" I whisper horrified.

Francis turns to me, his eyes sharp. "He is betraying no-one. He is simply handing over traitors to the king's lieutenant, to be dealt with according to the law of the kingdom."

"They are innocent, Francis," I say, my eyes welling with tears. "They are only guilty of being fools at best or callous towards the beliefs of others at worst. This is not something to die for." I go to him and place my hand on his shoulder. "Reprimand them, but please don't burn them. You know this is the truth..."

"I know this is the truth?" He cuts me off, his eyes narrowing. "What these reformists are spouting? Margaret, do you really think that I have indulged this movement, indulged *your* interest in it, because I believe in it?"

I feel as though he has reached out and slapped me across the face. "I thought that..." I pause, suddenly unsure of what I had thought. "You seemed to...consider it," I finally say.

"I have tolerated it because it has suited my purpose. It has helped to keep those wretched scholars at the Sorbonne in check and it has given me an opportunity to have some of the most talented minds at my court. But now it would seem that this movement is threatening my hold on my throne and my kingdom and it is time for me to make a decisive stand."

"You cannot burn people for following their conscience," I say, shaking my head in disbelief. I feel a sudden dawning of realisation. It is as though I have stared at a face my entire life and am only just seeing it. It is as though I am standing before a stranger. I feel as though I do not know my brother anymore.

"Following their conscience?" he says, his face twisting in scorn. "If I were to allow every man and his dog to follow their conscience, then where would I be? Facing a revolution against my throne, that's where. I want absolute control, Margaret. I want my subjects to bow to me and my divine right as king. A divine right conferred upon me by the pope and the church. Should I, even for a moment, flirt with this reformist foolishness, I would endanger my crown and my kingdom, and I will not do that. Not for any amount of proffered grace. My divine right as king is sustained by the church and I will not jeopardise that!"

I stare at him for a moment and then shake my head. "You cannot kill them," I say.

"I am the King of France. I can do whatever I want and you, sister, will stand by my side and smile and bear it."

I shake my head. "I cannot, Francis. I cannot sanction this. I cannot let you do it."

"Let me do it? And who are you to stand in my way?"

We are silent. Staring each other down like opponents in the lists, lances at the ready, aimed to pierce through the heart. After a long moment, Francis drags a hand across his face and gestures towards the door. "Leave me, Margaret," he says, his voice a whisper.

The struggle that is taking place in my heart is mirrored on his face. We are so intricately intertwined, our hearts so closely knit, that neither of us can bear the thought of anything separating us, yet I know that a sword hangs over us. The sword of the gospel, the sword of the Spirit, which is the Word of God, and with a single decisive stroke, it will tear us apart, separating two hearts that have long beat as one.

I stay in Paris for a few more days. The affair of the placards, as they are calling it, has turned into a nightmare. Enraged Catholic scholars at the Sorbonne call for the extermination of every reformist. The masses of Paris are in agreement. Fear hangs in the air like a putrid stench and no-one feels safe. Rumours abound like weeds. They say that the reformists have gone mad, they say that they will murder faithful Catholics in their beds, but worst of all, they say that reformists have hatched a plot to murder the king. No-one is safe, they say, for if the king himself is not safe in his bedchamber, how can anyone else be?

Francis refuses to see me and I am glad. I do not think that I could face him with all of this going on. Our relationship feels as fragile as a small child's bones.

Then the burnings begin. Morin, my brother's lieutenant, has taken every reformist he can lay his hands on in Paris and condemned them to the flames. They come like sheep to the slaughter, not only to be killed but tortured. The executioners place drenched wood in the pyres so that the smoke billows and the flames singe but do not rage. The reformists die in agony, but I hear they die in peace. I am loath that they should die at all. Why can we not be more tolerant of the new teachings? How can we reckon the cost of what we are doing now? Will France be ready to pay when she is held accountable? Selfishly, I pray that I will not live to see it happen.

They burn them for days on end, in every corner of the city, not only as an example but also as an assurance. The burnings communicate that the reformists who dared to speak so boldly against the mass are no longer a threat. The city lies silent, smacking her lips under a thick pall of smoke. Paris is satisfied, sated. She has torn off her pound of flesh and seems to take quiet pride in it. My brother most of all. Every burning has taken place at his command.

Almost overnight, people realise just how many reformists have been among us. Artisans, writers, poets, theologians, scholars and courtiers—the very cream of France—have all disappeared. Some to the flames and others to a life in exile. There is a gaping hole in the heart of Paris where these men and women once stood but that doesn't seem to matter. There are others to fill those spaces. Paris will not mourn their loss, just as no-one mourns for stray dogs who have died in the winter.

In all this, I feel as though the time for my own reckoning has come, for though Francis would never sacrifice me to the flames, he knows that he is burning those that I hold dear. This knowledge drives a wedge between us that I fear might never be removed.

January, 1535

It has been months since the affair of the placards, but despite all the blood and burning, Francis is not satisfied. I have been summoned to Paris again. My brother wants me. I come back to the city trembling, for I cannot fathom what he wants me for. I go to him in his privy chamber and close the door. His back is to me and he is very still. I wait. Surely he knows I have just entered his room.

"I am preparing an act of final ablution," he says quietly.

"Ablution?" I ask.

"The church has demanded that the sins of the reformists be expiated by blood."

"And has it not shed enough?" I ask, an edge creeping into my voice. "Did it not burn and burn till Paris was thick with the stench of men and women roasting in the flames?"

He turns then, his eyes cold and hard. "Are you not one of us, Margaret?" he asks.

"I am not taking sides, Francis," I say. "But surely there is no need for more bloodshed?"

"How can you say you are not taking sides, Margaret? You are steeped in reformist thought and have protected its proponents. Have you not already taken sides?"

"No-one deserves to die just because their views do not align with those of the majority," I say quietly.

"Margaret, you have been safe until now because you are my sister, but you are not considering the influence of your actions upon the sovereignty of my throne. Do not think, sister, that you can go on without consequences."

"Then burn me!" I say rashly, weary of his veiled threats. But then I continue, desperate to get through to him. "Please listen to me, Francis. You have done enough. Sacrificed enough. Surely the church cannot demand more?"

He studies me and I hold myself still, meeting his gaze. "We are going to have a day of reconsecration," he says. "A return to the ways of the church. France will recommit herself wholeheartedly to the old religion. We will no longer countenance reform."

"Then France will be poorer for it," I say sadly.

He shakes his head. "France will return to her roots and you will return to yours. I want you beside me as I do this, Margaret."

"What will you do, Francis?" I ask, and he tells me, recounting each step in detail. I feel the blood drain from my face and when he finishes I am trembling. "No," I say. "You cannot. *I cannot!*"

"You will," he says advancing on me, pinning me with his eyes. "You will because I command it. You will because I am your brother. You will because blood is thicker than any other bond. I command your allegiance."

"You have it, Francis," I say softly. "You have my love and my loyalty. Not because you command it but because I choose to give it to you. But while I give you my allegiance, I do not give you my will. You can never, *never* force me to violate my conscience. What you are proposing to do is wrong and no matter how much I love you, no matter how deep our bond is, I cannot do this with you."

"So you will allow this to tear us apart?"

"Francis," I say weighing my words. "These new teachings have opened my heart to the love of Christ and the beauty of salvation as nothing else has. I admit, my views on reform are not as strong as those of Calvin or Luther, but I believe in salvation by faith, I believe that every subject of France has the right to read the Bible in their own language, I believe in many of the new teachings," I pause and take a deep breath, "but above all, I believe that we, as rulers, must exercise tolerance. You cannot kill people because their views do not align with your own. That is madness and I cannot stand by and support you while you do it."

He looks at me as though I have been unmasked, as though I am not Margaret. He reaches out to hold my hand. "I need you," he says softly.

"And I need you," I nod. "But not at this cost."

I have read in the gospels, where our Lord said that He came to bring a sword. To set a man against his father and daughter against mother. Now I understand what He meant. It is not merely a sword of contention, it is a sword of separation, a sword of rending. A painful, slow dividing asunder of hearts and lives that have been bound so tightly together that neither knows where one begins and the other ends. It feels like a mortal wound and I do not know if I will survive. Looking at my brother I know that he feels as I do.

Days later they are ready for their spectacle. Till the last, Francis and I both hold out hope that the other will change their minds. We are both strong willed, we are both fervent in our devotions, but we have chosen separate paths.

I stand watching from a window in one of the galleries of the Louvre. It is daybreak and the sky is a haze of pink and grey. In the courtyard below me, the members of the procession are arranging themselves. Outside, beyond the gates and down as far as the riverbank, crowds line the streets. Eager, expectant, devout. It is the day when Paris and by extension, France, officially denounces the reformed faith and pledges itself wholeheartedly to Romanism. There is to be no opportunity for anyone to choose. The choice has already been made—by divine right of the king—and all his subjects are to obey. Reminders of the consequences of disobedience will be liberally scattered throughout the proceedings of the day.

Below I see the Bishop of Paris, John du Bellay, standing beneath a magnificent canopy of gold cloth, held up by my three young nephews and our cousin, the Duke of Vendome. They are all princes of the blood, all directly in line to the throne. The bishop carries a monstrance and his crimson robes billow about him.

Then I see my brother, stepping out of the great doors of the Louvre, coming to stand behind the bishop. He is dressed in black, bare-headed and carrying a single taper. This is how penitents dress, those who have wronged the church and the Holy Father. And today the King of France has chosen to dress like this, in a show of humility, repentance and submission.

Paris is in mourning for the occasion. As I look out over the city from where I stand, I can see great swathes of black cloth draped over houses and a single torch gleaming in every doorway in honour of the recently desecrated host. *Why must it be thus?* I think. *Why must it be a damnable offence to preach the Bible? Why is it wrong to preach salvation and grace and faith?*

The procession that has assembled in the courtyard of the palace moves forward to the great gates and I watch as they are joined by a throng of bishops, resplendent in their crimson robes and hats. The people trail behind them, eyes downcast in penitence. And then, in the distance, I see smoke and I know what it is. My brother has commanded the burning of reformists on every street corner as the procession passes. Today there will be a sacrifice of blood, a human sacrifice.

My sister-in-law, the queen, joins the procession then. Pale-faced, she casts a glance behind her and sees me watching. She turns her head. I watch from the window as the procession makes its way through the city. It pauses at every pyre and the smoke rises from a dozen altars where martyrs are spilling their blood for their faith. Francis wanted me to join this procession. To march, as my sister-in-law Eleanor is doing, pale-faced and sombre. To watch as they set alight reformist after reformist on every wretched street corner. I cannot. I will not.

I do not know how long I stand there, watching in the abandoned gallery, lost in thought. What seems like hours later, I see them making their way back to the palace. My family. My brother, my nephews, my sister-in-law and my husband. They come through the courtyard and one by one they glance up and see me. Francis holds my gaze the longest.

When I first began corresponding with William Briconnet all those years ago, I did not stop to count the cost. The new teachings drew me like a moth to a flame, yet never, for even a moment, did I think that I would be burnt. I have seen this flame scorch and incinerate others who have gotten too close, but I have not been singed. It has not touched me, until today. Today it has cost me something to say no. Though my body has not been given to the flames, my heart has been carved in two. Standing for what I believe in has severed a bond that I fear can never be restored.

I turn slowly away from the window. Away from the smoking pyres, the milling throngs, the crimson robes and I think: *If I were given the choice once more, I would do nothing differently.*

Margaret of Navarre (1492–1549) was born Margaret of Angouleme. She was educated alongside her brother Francis and was fluent in a number of languages. She was a prolific writer and wrote both sacred and secular literature. Her book The Mirror of a Sinful Soul, *which was a treatise on justification by faith, influenced many other women around Europe. Notably, the young Princess Elizabeth of England translated the work into English and presented it to her step-mother Queen Katherine Parr as a Christmas gift. Margaret actively sheltered reformist thinkers and offered men like John Calvin and Jacques Lefevre refuge on several occasions. Thanks to her influence, many young women in her sphere embraced the teachings of the Reformation, especially the principle of justification by faith. Among them were Princess Renee of France, who would later become the Duchess of Ferrara, and Philiberta of Savoy who was married to Julian de Medici, the younger brother of Pope Leo X.*

4

Louise de Coligny
DAUNTLESS

Delft, the Low Countries
July 10, 1584

I glance up from my plate and I see him standing in the doorway of the great hall. It is his eyes that arrest me, stripping away my smile like a knife slicing flesh away from bone. Immediately, I search his face for signs of familiarity but there are none. He is a stranger to me. I do not know him, but I know his eyes. There is something in their expression that brings a flood of memories back to me. Memories of summer and bells and a great cathedral.

"Louise?" the voice of my sister-in-law Elizabeth wrenches me back into the present. "What is it?" she asks. "What has happened?"

I open my mouth to speak, but nothing comes out. I stare at her blankly, struggling to put my reaction into words.

"Who is that man?" I finally manage to whisper to my husband. William glances up at me then and follows my gaze towards the entrance to the great hall. When his eyes light on the man in question, I see a flicker of recognition in them.

"Ah, Francois," he says softly.

The man's eyes meet his and they exchange a moment of silent communication. William nods and gestures towards the door. The man responds with a nod of his own, bows and then retreats.

"That is Francois Guyon and he is here for a passport," William says.

"A passport?" I echo uncomprehendingly.

"He is a messenger of mine, my dear," William says. "A trusted spy who serves us at the Spanish court."

My mind struggles to comprehend my husband's words and all I can see in my mind is Paris. Paris in the summer of 1572. Paris, just before my entire life shattered and fell apart.

"He is sinister," I say, twisting my fingers together to keep them from trembling.

William reaches out and pats my hand reassuringly. "He is perfectly trustworthy," he tells me. "He has proven his loyalty to me, so much so that I count him among my most faithful servants."

But his words do nothing to comfort me. My face betrays my concern and he chuckles, pushing away from his place at the table and rising to his feet. "You worry too much, my love," he says smiling.

My eyes snap into focus at his words. He bows to us, then turns and begins to make his way across the great hall towards the wide doors, towards Francois Guyon. But as I watch him stride away from me, all I can see is another man, at another time, speaking the same words.

Paris, France

August 18, 1572

We are all standing around waiting. Fanning ourselves like life-sized dolls, dressed in velvet, silk and brocade, and waxy in the afternoon heat. We cannot even open a window for fear of the masses. They have lined the streets below, thronging the banks of the Seine, peering up at the windows of the Palace of the Louvre, hoping, no doubt, to catch a glimpse of a courtier or noble or even the groom himself. But none of them are anywhere in sight.

It is just us ladies. Sweating, fanning, murmuring. The mood in the city below is strange. A perfect juxtaposition of emotion. Excitement laced with a low thrum of sullen disappointment. Joy over the impending royal wedding but with an undercurrent of surliness because Huguenots are involved.

Whatever else she may be, Paris is a Romanist maiden, and she is not pleased at being forced to open her gates to such a great influx of Huguenots, no matter who we are or what our rank. There is a part of me that is afraid to step out of the palace. What if someone hurls a rock? What if someone brandishes a gun? We have the king's word that we are safe, but these days the king's word means precious little. I feel as though we are players in a masque and soon the pretence will fall away and reveal the faces that lurk beneath the painted smiles. Despite the sweltering weather, a shiver passes over me and I turn away from the window where I have been standing.

"Do you think this will bring peace?" The sound of the soft voice behind me makes me turn, and I reach out a hand and grasp the cool fingers extended towards me. Catherine comes to stand in the window embrasure beside me. She scans the streets below. "Do you think so, Louise?" she asks.

I don't really know how to answer her, but I sense that she is desperate for reassurance, so I smile and say gently, "I pray so." There is nothing else I can say.

Catherine is only thirteen. Her father, the old King of Navarre, is long dead. Her mother, the queen, passed to her rest not two months ago and now her beloved brother, the current King of Navarre, is about to be married. Her life is in turmoil and, what is worse, after all the tedious jostling that has surrounded this marriage, no-one knows if it will bring peace. We all hope that it will, but who can say for certain?

"My lady mother . . ." Catherine swallows hard and I squeeze her hand. "My lady mother would never have consented to this marriage if she didn't believe it would bring about some good," she whispers.

"Your Highness," I say, "we are all praying that your brother's marriage will bring peace to France. It is our fondest hope."

Perhaps our last hope, I think to myself.

I have lived in the midst of war for so long that it has become a second skin. The constant tension, the constant fear, the shadow of death that hangs over us like a pall. It is my birthright for so many reasons. My father is a son of one of the great noble houses of the kingdom. He is also Admiral of France. He was made Admiral before I was born, then when I was not yet two, he was taken as a prisoner of war during the battle of St Quentin. During his time as a prisoner, he read the Bible and accepted the reformed faith. His religious inclinations did not affect his position as Admiral of France, for he was not the only noble of high rank to have embraced the new reformist doctrines. When Papa came home from St Quentin he was a new man, and our lives were never the same again.

I remember the changes that took place in our home in Chatillon-sur-Loing. The chapel was stripped bare, the pictures of saints whisked off the walls, the great rood taken down and the monstrance quietly disposed of. Then instead of the smell of incense and candles, there was a lingering smell of fresh paint. Instead of an altar, there was a table with a Bible on it. Instead of the chapel bells tolling the hours for mass, we gathered morning and evening to read psalms and listen to a sermon. We prayed directly to God instead of invoking the saints and we no longer passed beads through our fingers in a never-ending line. I grew up in a Huguenot home and I am grateful for it. But our faith has exacted a heavy price.

Three years after we accepted the reformed faith, war broke out. There was a massacre of Huguenots at Vassy. My father's brothers, Odet and Andelot, rode up to our home and closeted themselves with my father all afternoon. When everyone had retired for the night, I lay in bed wide awake and listening. I was seven and knew enough to understand that something wasn't right. I remember peeling off the bed clothes and tiptoeing past my sleeping nurse. I scuttled down the hallway, pausing at the door to my mother's bedchamber. I was about to open the door and slip inside when I heard voices. I pressed my ear to the door and listened, curious. I could hear my mother crying and my father's voice, a low murmur speaking to her. I pushed my ear more firmly against the door and strained to listen. I could make out my mother's voice then, the words muffled but distinct.

"How can you rest comfortably in your bed when your Huguenot brothers lie butchered in a field?" My mother was sobbing. My father's voice rumbled low again, but I couldn't make out his words.

"We must do something!" my mother cried out. "We cannot stand by and let this injustice continue! Why should they be slaughtered? Because they dared to uplift the Bible? Because they dared to worship God according to the dictates of their conscience?"

Then I heard my father's voice, no longer quiet but clear and piercing in the stillness of the night. "Will you then lay your hand to your heart and say that you are willing to bear the cost?" I heard my father's footfalls as he paced the room. "Are you willing to lose everything? Our houses? Our lands? Are you willing to watch your husband join the ranks of the dead who are mutilated in the fields? Are you willing to see your sons join those ranks? Have you counted the cost, Charlotte?"

There was a long silence and then I heard my mother's voice. "I have," she said quietly. "I am willing to lose my life and the lives of those I love for Christ, Gaspard. If I were not, then I am not worthy of my calling."

That night changed the course of our lives. Though it was my uncles who asked my father to take up arms, it was my mother who sent him to war. My mother, my brave mother, who counted the cost and found that the truth was worth the price it exacted.

But after ten years of fighting, there is now a great desire for peace. We have lost so much. Surely, surely there is cause to parley for peace? And so this marriage has been negotiated. It is a desperate attempt by the Queen Mother, Catherine de Medici, to broker peace, to bring the warring factions together. And so here we are. Here in Paris for the wedding. The wedding of Henry de Bourbon, King of Navarre, and Princess Marguerite de Valois, sister to the King of France. He is a staunch Huguenot and one of the most powerful, being a prince of the blood with a claim to the French throne. She is an ardent Catholic, the daughter of a king.

So we have all come to Paris to watch them wed. We hope and pray that somehow this union, forged in the very midst of bloodshed, will stanch the flow and bring it all to an end. But only God knows if it will come to anything.

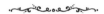

The doors to our chamber open and the men file in. Catherine immediately dashes to greet her brother, the groom. Henry is nineteen, just two years older than I am, and we have known each other since we were children.

Behind him, in Henry's train, is my father—Admiral of France, leader of the Huguenot forces, handsome, strong, brave and one of the most godly men I know. He is also one of the most wanted men in France. Not wanted by the king, for he is a close adviser to His Majesty, but rather wanted by the Catholic faction of this religious war that has waged for the better part of a decade. They would give much to see him dead.

Beside Papa is my husband Charles. Charles is a soldier, who has faithfully fought beside my father for much of this war, but he is also a diplomat and a peacemaker. It is an unlikely combination but one that makes him an incredibly safe man to be around. We grew up together, but we have been married only a year. I smile at them both, these two men who completely own my heart, and I gravitate towards them like a magnet.

"Ah, Louise," Papa kisses me on both cheeks. "You are looking lovely, my dear." I smile and dip my head. Charles grins at me almost wolfishly and I giggle, a blush rising up my neck.

We arrange ourselves into the train of the young King of Navarre and proceed through the gallery, down the stairs and out the doors of the great Palace of the Louvre. Once we are outside on the streets, we hear the restless murmur of the crowd begin to rise.

The *Garde Ecossaise*, the personal bodyguards of the king, accompany us as we make our way towards Notre Dame Cathedral, where the wedding is to be held. Henry is draped in yellow satin, his doublet and cape encrusted with pearls and diamonds. On either side of him are the bride's brothers, all except the King of France.

They too are swathed in satin and drenched in jewels. When the crowd catches sight of them, there is a cheer. The young princes wave and nod. There are shouts of "*Vive les Valois!*"—the name of their royal house. But there are no shouts for the groom or any of his entourage, just a low murmur of disapproval. I feel as though we are walking through a den of lions, their eyes following our every movement. I walk in Princess Catherine's train, and I keep my head down and my eyes on the ground before my feet. I dare not look at the crowd. I am still terrified of someone throwing a rock at my face.

When we reach the cathedral, I am struck by the sheer opulence of the building. A platform draped in gold cloth has been erected on the west side of the church. As we take our places and the bride's procession comes out to meet us, there is a roar from the crowd. The people of Paris love Princess Marguerite. She is their own; they cannot help but love her.

The bride and groom take their places facing one another. They make no move to touch or even look at each other. The princess' head is down, her eyes averted. Henry is swallowing convulsively. But it is not as if they are strangers. We are all related to one another, by birth or by marriage or both. It is not only in England that cousins marry cousins, the French can do that just as well.

Cardinal de Bourbon quietly recites their vows to them. When it is time for them to plight their troth, Henry, with a relieved look on his face, nods, says "I will" and is quickly done with it. The cardinal then turns to the princess and there is silence. At first, we all wonder if she has heard him. But then we notice the defiant tilt of her chin and the anger flashing in her eyes. Her mother and brother have forced her into this, and it is clear that she resents being sacrificed on the altar of the best interests of the kingdom. The silence stretches long, like a thick rope pulled taut. Henry shuffles and swallows again. There are murmurs in the crowd, stirrings among the Huguenots and raised eyebrows among the bride's relatives.

Then there is an exasperated snort and all eyes shift to the bride's oldest brother, the King of France. "*Oh, for heaven's sake, Margot!*" Charles hisses at his sister. Marching forward, he plants his large hand against the back of her head and pushes it forward and downwards. He then glares at the cardinal. "She is in agreement. Proceed," he snaps.

Princess Marguerite raises her head and glares bitterly at Henry, who looks at her in shock.

The cardinal drones on. And then it is all done. The ceremony is finished, and the bride and her family and friends make their way towards the doors of the cathedral to hear the wedding mass. Without the groom. For that has been a stipulation of the marriage contract. She may have her mass, but she may not expect her husband to attend.

The sonorous bells of Notre Dame start pealing, signalling to Paris that their princess is wed. The sound echoes through the cathedral, and birds scatter from the belfry and wheel into the sky, a plume of grey and white against the brilliant blue. At other times, the ringing of the bells is a joyful sound, but now it seems to fill the air with tension, like a warning, an alarm.

And that is when I feel it. The escalating throb of disapproval in the crowd before us. I cast my eyes over the sea of Parisian faces looking up at the platform where we Huguenots are now standing alone. Their eyes arrest me, stripping me of my sense of security. Not a single face is familiar. They are all strangers. But as I watch them watching me, I think that I shall never forget their eyes, not as long as I live. They glare back at me with hatred, barely leashed, smouldering like fire. Instinctively, I shrink against my husband and his arm curves around me, nestling me into his side. But it is a thin shield, for I know that if they decide to set upon us, they could tear us limb from limb and nothing could stop them.

August 22, 1572

I do not need to wait long for my fears of reprisal to materialise. Four days later, I am seated in the rooms of the newly married Princess Marguerite at the Louvre, when my husband Charles comes for me. When I see his face, my needlework falls to the floor and I spring up from my stool by the window.

"What is it?" I gasp. "What has happened?"

The entire room has gone still and every eye is fixed on me, but Charles does not speak. Instead, he gives a little shake of his head and, bowing to the ladies, he escorts me out of the presence chamber and into the hallway beyond.

He faces me, holding my hands, and says, "Louise, your father has been shot. He's..."

I feel my knees buckle beneath me. He holds me up and I suddenly want to scream. To rail at him and every foolish Huguenot man that thought that we would be safe here. Why have they brought us here? We have come to die. All of us.

"Louise," Charles shakes me gently. "My love, he is not dead."

I stare at him wide-eyed, tears streaming down my face. "Not dead?" I repeat.

"No." He wraps his arms around me and pulls me close. "He is alive. Thank God, the assassin's aim was poor."

But he will be back, I think. I pull away from Charles and search his face. "Who sent him?" I ask. "Did they apprehend him? If they did not, then he will be back. Or even if they did, then whoever sent the first one can also send another. We must leave. Charles, we must go back home, to Chatillon and then perhaps to La Rochelle, where we will be near the sea and safe." I am babbling and Charles is looking at me with a gentle smile.

"We are safe here," he says, and I look at him incredulously.

"We are not safe!" I cry out. "If we were, then no-one would have made an attempt on Papa's life."

"The king has given us his word that we are safe."

"The king?" I screech, my voice rising an octave, "The king's word is worthless!"

"*Louise*," he hisses, grabbing my arm and dragging me further down the hall, away from the halberdiers standing at the door. "Keep your voice down!"

"Why?" I ask. I cannot be reasoned with, I refuse to be reasoned with. It is their foolish reasoning that has brought us to this place and now I mean to tell them as much. My father, Charles, all the other Huguenot nobles, all of them have assured us that we will be safe in Paris and now look. Look at how safe we are.

"If they kill Papa...if they kill him, then where will we be? The entire Huguenot cause rests on Papa. He is the backbone of it all. If they cut him down, then we will be like chaff in the wind," I say, fresh tears spring into my eyes. "There will never be peace, Charles, don't you see? They will not rest until they have killed us all, until they have hacked up our bodies and left them to rot in the sun."

Charles gives me a little shake because I am now nearly hysterical. "*Arretez!*" he says, gently but firmly. "Louise, stop this. You worry too much, my love. The king has given us his word. As much as anywhere in this world is safe, we are safe here."

I gape at him in open-mouthed disbelief then. My husband is the very measure of the eternal optimist and yet surely even he cannot possibly believe the words that are coming out of his mouth.

"We are not safe," I say slowly, like I am speaking to a child, and I see his jaw clench. "How can you say we are, when Papa has been shot?" My throat closes then and I am choked with emotion as I consider the grim reality before me. "Where will I be if they kill Papa? If they kill you?" I place my trembling hand against his cheek.

Sighing, he pulls me close once more. "You know, Louise," he says softly. "We cannot be *perfectly* secure anywhere on earth. Not even in Chatillon or La Rochelle. This is our legacy as Huguenots. We understand the risks and yet we take them because we believe that our cause is just, that it is worthy."

"I do not want to be a martyr's wife," I whisper miserably. "Or a martyr's daughter."

"What would your mother say?" he asks gently, pulling away to look down at my face.

"I am not my mother," I say, looking up at him. "I am not as brave as she was. I am not strong."

He frames my face with his hands and his expression turns serious. "You can be, Louise," he says, "if you look to Christ. Consider Him and the suffering He endured, then ask Him for courage and strength. With Him, you can be dauntless whatever storms lie ahead."

Charles takes me to see my father and I rush to his side sobbing. He gently murmurs in my ear and rubs my back like he did when I was a little girl and ran to him for comfort.

"We must leave, Papa," I implore him. "What if they try again? They will not miss twice."

"We cannot leave, Louise. There is still much to be done. We were on our way home from meetings with the Privy Council when the assassin shot at me. I cannot leave now."

I bury my face in his shoulder when I hear his words, a terrible dark foreboding falling over me. I know they will not stop. I saw it in their faces at the wedding. France is Romanist. The people are Romanist. It is as though they have faithfully inscribed every insult or injury Romanism has suffered over the past decades in a long scroll. Recording every sermon preached against the mass, every pamphlet denouncing the authority of the pope, every bill of receipt made out for the purchase of a French Bible. It is as though they have kept an account of it all and now they have come to make a reckoning, and we must pay for it in blood.

"They will not stop until you are dead," I tell him, lifting my head to search his face.

"Then I will have given my life for the cause of Christ and I cannot ask for a better end than that," he touches my face and smiles. "I cannot run and hide."

I know he cannot. Not now, not after so many years of fighting and praying.

"Then I will ask God for courage and strength," I say resignedly, because there is nothing else to say.

Charles comes to my side and ushers me out of the room then, murmuring that my father needs to rest. We go out into the little private garden at the back of the house and sit on a bench underneath a tree. Birdsong fills the air, along with the sounds of Paris beyond the walls, vibrant and alive on a mid-summer's day.

"You must stay at the palace," he finally says after a prolonged silence.

"No," I reply. I fist my hands in my lap and stare him down defiantly. "I want to stay here, in our lodgings."

Charles and I have rented a house next door to Papa for the duration of our stay in Paris and though I spend time at court during the day, I always return home in the evenings.

"Louise," he begins, facing me down, prepared to do battle.

"Charles, please," I beg. "I cannot leave you and Papa, not after what has happened today."

He jumps to his feet and begins to pace before me. "That is precisely why I want you at court, safe and sound."

"But you yourself just told me that we are safe! The king himself has sent a contingent of the *Garde Ecossaise* and then there are the halberdiers of Navarre. How could I possibly be more safe inside the palace?"

Charles sighs. "Beloved, I know what I told you. You were frantic about leaving Paris and I meant that the danger here is much the same as anywhere else. There is no cause for all of us to run back to Chatillon in terror. The talks in progress are too important for us to leave now. You heard your father. The risk that there might be another attempt on his life is a risk he is willing to take. It is a risk he takes every day, regardless of where he is. And the king *has* done everything possible to ensure our safety here. But if something were to happen, your father and I would both prefer you to be away from it all."

"Do you know who it was?" I ask, picturing the assassin's attempt on Papa's life.

Charles shakes his head. "No, we had just walked through the gates of the Louvre and were walking down the street when the shots rang out. Your father pointed to where he thought they had come from, but when we ran to investigate there was no-one there."

"But you have your suspicions?" I press. Charles studies me for a moment, and I know he is wondering how much he should tell me. "I have grown up around war," I remind him. "There is nothing that you can say to me that will shock me."

"There are rumours that it was the Duke of Guise," he finally says.

I am not surprised. "He still thinks Papa is responsible for the assassination of his father," I say softly. Charles nods.

This war that we find ourselves fighting began quietly, like a cauldron of water slowly coming to the boil. Persecution of the Huguenots increased gradually, but we cannot only blame the Romanists for this. We Huguenots were responsible for a handful of foolish debacles that only served to fan the flames of persecution. But the catalyst came when Duke Francois of Guise—the father of the current duke, Henry—massacred an entire congregation of Huguenots while they were at worship in the village of Vassy ten years ago.

It was after this that my uncles came to our home and begged my father to lead the Huguenots in an armed resistance. Papa was the obvious choice. As Admiral of France, he had control of the navy and every port, he wielded great power, but he was also completely devoted to the cause of reform. It was difficult for Papa to take up arms, difficult for him to become embroiled in civil war, but he has fought valiantly.

The most significant moment of this war, for Papa personally, was during the siege of Orleans a year after the war began. It was here that a Huguenot assassinated Duke Francois of Guise. It was an act of retaliation, revenge for what he had done at Vassy. The assassin, Jean de Poltrot, was captured and he claimed that Papa had been involved in the conspiracy to assassinate the Duke. It was, of course, a lie. Papa denied it and later de Poltrot retracted it, claiming that he was mistaken, but the damage was done. The Duke's son, Henry, fixed on Papa as a mark for his anger and grief. Henry vowed revenge upon Papa and our whole house. He has waited a long time to exact that revenge.

"Henry must be angry, Charles," I reflect. "Not only does he believe that Papa was behind his father's assassination, but he is also in love with Princess Marguerite and she is in love with him. Her ladies were whispering about it at court. And now they have married her off to the King of Navarre to broker peace with the Huguenots. The Duke of Guise already hated Huguenots and now he has even more cause to."

"All the more reason for you to stay at the palace away from your father for now," Charles replies, coming back to the subject we have been arguing about.

"I am not leaving," I tell him adamantly. "Please Charles. I can't be away from you both. If you and Papa are willing to accept the risk of staying here, then I am willing to accept the risk of staying with you."

He stands in front of me, studying my face. I can see the wheels turning in his sharp mind, assessing the risks, calculating the variables, like a commander on a battlefield trying to keep his soldiers safe. Finally, he nods. "I will station extra men at the gates."

Then he sits beside me once more and reaches for my hands, lacing his fingers through mine. "I believe," he begins, pausing to find the right words. "I believe that Jesus considered our salvation to be a cause worth risking His life for, a cause worth suffering and grieving for. The battle we are fighting is for that same cause. The people of France have a right to choose who they will worship and how they will worship. They have a right to a free conscience."

"There are some who would say that freedom of conscience is for those who desire a republic, not for the subjects of a king," I say, a small smile playing across my lips.

He grins. "Then perhaps we are republicans."

"You would never impugn the authority of the king!" I exclaim, horrified that he would say such a thing.

"No," he concedes, "but the king cannot touch my conscience. It is not his place to tell me how to worship God, nor is it the place of the pope. No man can stand as God over another."

"They will kill us all as traitors and heretics," I say, as I realise the implications of our beliefs for the established hierarchies of France.

He looks at me for a long moment. "And if we give our lives, then we are doing no less than our Saviour," he says softly.

"But will the sacrifice be worth it?" I ask.

"What price would you pay for a free conscience?" he counters, his intense gaze burning into mine.

"Not the blood of my father or my husband," I say, a bitter edge creeping into my voice.

"You can only answer for your own blood, my love," he says, his eyes softening. "You cannot answer for mine."

"Even so," I counter, "I must still bear the weight of the choices you make."

"That is the cost of love, of freedom."

We stare at each other for a long time, mulling over our words and the intricacies of freedom and choice and love and risk and pain.

Charles escorts me back to our lodgings later in the afternoon. When he is gone, I sit on the small window seat in our bedroom, gazing out over the Rue de Betizy where we are staying. The streets of Paris are alive and the air is heady with the smells of summer, but there is a terrible storm rolling through my soul and I long for comfort. I long for peace, and there is only one place that I know to find it. I have brought my little book of psalms to the window with me and now I open it.

When I was a little girl and in need of comfort, my mother would gather me in her lap and read a psalm and pray with me. Now my mother is gone but the Word of God remains. I open the well-worn cover and leaf through the pages, hungry for words that can offer me hope and light. My roving eyes fall on the words of the twenty-third psalm: "Yea though I walk through the valley of the shadow of death, I will fear no evil: for thou art with me; thy rod and thy staff they comfort me."

I press my eyes tightly shut. I do not want to think of the valley of the shadow of death, but I know that even now I am walking through it. I sense it, the stench of the reaper's breath hot on my neck. For a moment panic seizes me and I feel trapped, my lungs struggling to draw in a breath. I feel as though my fear will overwhelm me as countless possibilities swirl in my mind.

We are surrounded by Romanists with whom we have been at war for a decade. We only have the king's word that we are safe, and I do not doubt, whatever Charles and Papa might say, that the king would sell us to the highest bidder to keep his hold on the throne if the need arose. The people of Paris despise us; it would not take much to stir them. Every main gate in the city is shut; only two of the smaller gates are open to admit goods. If they wanted to kill us, it would be like shooting fish in a barrel. Yet I now see that moving my father would be foolish. His injuries would only worsen. He might catch a fever and die before we have reached home. We have no choice but to stay.

My heart pounds and my anxiety only increases as I think about these things. More and more, I come to feel as though we have walked into a trap with our eyes wide open. My trembling fingers comb the pages of my little book and I find the twenty-eighth psalm. Immediately, I latch onto the words and they become the cry of my heart, directed in a fervent stream towards heaven: "Unto thee will I cry, O Lord my rock; be not silent to me: lest, if thou be silent to me, I become like them that go down into the pit. Hear the voice of my supplications, when I cry unto thee, when I lift up my hands toward thy holy oracle."

I know in the depths of my heart that what awaits me is nothing less than a baptism of fire and blood. Closing the Scriptures, I sink to the floor, hands clasped, eyes tightly shut. I know that there is only one Person I can turn to now.

August 24, 1572

I have prepared myself for heartache and even death, but nothing has prepared me for a bloodbath. Two days after Papa is shot, on the eve of St Bartholmew's Day, I awake with a start to the sound of church bells pealing. I bolt upright looking over at Charles. He too has sat up and is flinging the covers aside. He goes to the window, and when he opens it, the haunting melody of the bells, ringing out in the darkness, fills the room like an omen.

"What is it?" I whisper through the darkness, watching his still form in the puddle of moonlight streaming through the open window.

"It is the song of the bells of St Germain l'Auxerrois," he whispers back. It is the church nearest to us. In the distance, across the city, we hear other bells begin to add their notes to the still night. Then we hear a sharp crack not far from us and we both jump. Immediately, Charles strides away from the window and begins to dress.

"What was that?" I ask, though I know in my heart what it was.

"Gunshot," he says grimly, and I watch him reach for his pistol, which he has kept beside the bed.

"What are you doing?" I ask him, wide-eyed with fear. "Where are you going?"

He turns to me then and I can see the hard line of his jaw.

"They have come for us," he says simply, quietly. He holds out his hands to me and I scramble across the bed and go to him. "Listen to me, Louise," he says, framing my face with his hands. "They have come for your father and if they reach him, they will think to take all of us. You are not safe. None of us are. I am going to your father's side now. Lock the front door behind me, then get dressed. I want you to leave through the back door and make your way across the river. There is a company of Huguenot troops on the other side. Go to them, tell them who you are and get them to give you a horse and an escort, then ride as fast as you can to Chatillon. Take your step-mother and your brothers and leave France."

I begin to shake my head as his words sink in. "No!" I say. "No, I cannot leave you and Papa. I cannot!"

"You must. Listen to me, Louise. Listen," he insists, as I continue shaking my head. "Once they have taken your father, they will come for your brothers. You have to warn them. You have to make sure they are safe, do you understand me? You have to make sure the family is safe, and right now your only safety is in exile. Cross the border into Switzerland, go to Basel and find your cousin Guy. He will give you refuge."

He is so calm. Like a commander on a battlefield. From outside the window, we hear shouts and the drumbeat of hooves heavy against the cobbles.

"I need you to be brave," he says softly. "You are the daughter of a commander, the wife of a soldier. You are a Coligny, Louise, but more than all that, you are a Huguenot. You know that this is our legacy.

With our last breath we will fight for freedom. And if we must wade through blood and fire to remain faithful, then we will do it."

His words sink deep into my soul and I know he is right. I think of my mother, of the many women who have gone before me, willingly sacrificing their husbands and fathers and brothers to a cause that is dear to their hearts. In war, it is the men who take to the field, but it is the women who reap the harvest of their blood. And now it is my turn. It is my turn to stand tall, to bid my husband farewell, to let my father go and find a way to save my brothers. I fling my arms around Charles and cling to him. I may never see him again and I feel in that moment that my heart is splintering into a million pieces. But I also know that he is right. I must be brave. Gently, he disentangles himself from my embrace, presses a kiss to my forehead and grabs my hand. He presses his sheathed knife into my palm and my fingers curl around the cold hilt.

After I have locked the door behind him, I run upstairs and get dressed. Through the window, I can now hear shrieks and wails. I can hear hoofbeats thundering down our street, men shouting, banging on doors. I know they have come for my father. I know they are next door, and I know that this time they will not miss. They will kill him in his bed while he lies there helpless and vulnerable, and they will then kill every other man who stands with him.

I dare not look down into the street below for fear of what I might see. I grab my book of psalms and the knife Charles has given me and throw on my hooded cape. Silently, I slink out the back door of our quarters and into the night. The alley behind the house is empty. Mentally, I map out my steps. I need to get across the river.

I walk towards the main thoroughfare of the Rue de Betizy, thinking that I might take it down to the Louvre and then make my way to the river from there. Reaching the end of the alley, I am about to step onto the road to cross, when I see a man just a few yards away from me, directly in front of my father's quarters. He is tall, made even taller by the great height of his war horse. The horse is restless, wheeling and prancing, but the man holds him firm. I freeze, willing the man not to notice me.

"Behme, is it done?" he calls out, and immediately I recognise his voice. It is Henry, the Duke of Guise.

"Yes, your grace! someone calls from the house

"Throw him down that I may see," the Duke calls back. After a short pause, there is a grunt and a dark shape tumbles onto the cold cobblestones at the feet of the Duke's horse. It is a body, soft and mangled under the cool light of the moon.

"It is Coligny," the Duke confirms flatly.

I press my fist to my mouth and swallow down the vomit that is rising rapidly. My Papa. My brave Papa. I am so tempted, in that moment to sink to the ground and give way to my grief, or to rush up to the Duke of Guise, seated on his wretched horse, and sink my knife into his thigh. I hardly know which, my pain is too great. But then I remember a psalm, a psalm that I have often read, and I turn my eyes heavenward in a silent and desperate prayer: "Unto thee, O Lord, do I lift up my soul. O my God, I trust in thee: let me not be ashamed, let not mine enemies triumph over me."

No matter the depth of my outrage, I know that I am no match for those who have lifted their hands against me and mine. My only refuge is in God and there, in that cold, dark alleyway, I lay my case before the Judge of all the earth. I know His ways are just and that there will be justice for my Papa.

Clinging to God with every shred of my mental strength, I force my feet to keep moving. As I move through the shadows, I see them dragging screaming Huguenots out of houses and slaughtering them like animals. Men, women, children, infants in their mother's arms. This must be what it was like when Herod ordered the massacre of the innocents, and yet somehow it is worse. Much worse. They did not just come for my father. They came for us all.

I manage to make it through the city, across the river and then safely to the Huguenot soldiers. I cannot erase what I have seen and it replays in my mind as I ride like a mad woman through the French countryside, a single Huguenot soldier at my side: the twisted faces of the Romanists, their eyes wild with rage, Papa's body, the faces of the innocents. And above it all, I hear the constant ringing of the bells—the bells which began with the mournful song of the bells at St Germain l'Auxerrois and spread throughout the city, till even the great bells of Notre Dame and the Palais de Justice took on their metre.

Chatillon-sur-Loing, France
August 26, 1572

We ride through the night and then stop at an inn as dawn begins to peek over the horizon. The soldier who is with me speaks to the innkeeper and negotiates an exchange of horses. We leave our mounts at the inn, take on fresh horses and keep going. When we ride into the courtyard at our home in Chatillon, we have ridden the horses nearly to death. They are lathered and foaming. I scream for the grooms and they come at a run, helping me dismount and holding me up when I nearly collapse on the ground.

"My brother," I say, grasping the groom's arm. "Fetch my brother."

They usher me into the great hall and help me into a chair. My entire body is quivering. I have not slept in two days and I have almost constantly been on a horse. The exhaustion is breaking down the thin grasp I have on my composure. I dare not think of Charles. I dare not or I fear that I shall go mad.

When Francois comes into the room, I stumble towards him, throw myself into his arms and sob. Loud, long wails of despair that bring my step-mother and my other brother Charles running. Francois cannot make sense of anything I am saying and finally he says sharply, "Louise! Stop this and tell me what has happened."

It is enough to wake me from my grief. The tale pours out of me then and I watch as the faces around me go pale with shock and grief. But we have not long to indulge our sorrow. Francois hands me to my step-mother and then begins to bark orders.

We decide to go to Bern and then on to Basel to my cousin Guy, where we hope to find refuge. It takes us two days to prepare. Two long and agonising days, where more reports of the St Bartholomew's Day massacre begin to trickle through to us. Just before we are to leave, I receive news that Charles is dead.

When we arrive in Bern we are all swathed in mourning, our black attire stiff and unyielding in the summer breeze. Fingering my widow's veil, I realise that I have become what I never aspired to be at the age of seventeen: both a widow and an orphan all at once. We eventually arrive in Basel at my cousin Guy's home and he gives us refuge. Myself, my step-mother and my brothers. We have very few possessions, but we are alive and we have each other and that is enough.

Basel, Switzerland

Spring, 1573

When we are in Basel, the Crown confiscates our assets and denounces us as heretics. They write to us to say that they will give us back our land and welcome us home to France if we are willing to renounce our faith. We write back to tell them that they can have our land but that our consciences will remain safe in the hands of God, where they belong. We will not acknowledge the mass, we will not renounce the Bible, but above all we will live and die free.

I finally feel I am able to grieve when I reach my cousin. I take out the letters that Papa and Charles have written to me in the past. I have brought these with me from Chatillon and now I read them, tears running down my face unhindered. I allow my heart to break, allow the pain of loss to sear me and engulf me all at once. I open my book and read psalm after psalm. I feel an affinity to King David. It is as though I have looked into his soul and he into mine; his words are mine. I understand their depths. Pain has a way of introducing us to realities that we might have otherwise never considered, dimensions of life that would have forever remained sealed to us had pain not opened a portal to them and showed us the way inside.

My losses have turned me to Calvary. The twenty-second psalm echoes in my soul and I know that Jesus understands my heart. He has walked through the very valley I now traverse, and I can place my feet in His footprints and know that there is light at the end of this journey. It is as though the very heart of God has been laid bare before me through the medium of my trials. God knows the pain of separation and loss and I feel His hand in mine.

In Paris, before the massacre, I was terrified of loss. I thought it would leave me unable to breathe or live. I thought I could not bear the pain. But now, in the depths of my grief I see the heart of God and I need see no more; it is enough for now.

Delft, the Low Countries
July 10, 1584

I watch my husband as he makes his way out of the great hall, my heart still beating fast. William is the Prince of Orange, and he was my father's ally and friend before the massacre. He is a champion of truth and freedom and, because of that, Spain has put a bounty on his reformist head and every gun in Romanist Europe is trained on him.

As he goes through the doors, I suddenly realise what is familiar about the eyes of the stranger—the spy, Francois Guyon. They are the eyes of the Parisian mob who stood watching us all on Princess Marguerite's wedding day. The same mob that, only six days later, hacked every Huguenot they could lay their hands on to pieces.

As I realise this, I begin to move and my sister-in-law Elizabeth follows me. I am halfway to the doors when I hear a gunshot. A sharp crack that makes me jump. Immediately, I think of Paris and the bells of St Germain l'Auxerrois on the moonlit night when my first husband pressed his dagger into my hands and told me to run.

I run then, through the great double doors and out into the hall. It is as though I am in a dream. A nightmare. William is on the floor, slumped in an ever-widening pool of blood. I hear screaming and as I run to my husband's side, I realise the screams are my own. I crouch beside him and press the heel of my hand to one of the wounds on his chest but there is more than one and so much blood. I have never seen so much blood in my life.

I look up in desperation and see Elizabeth on the other side of my husband. She is screaming and sobbing and pressing her hand onto another wound in his chest. The man who has shot him, the familiar stranger, is across the room, his gun on the floor, his eyes gleaming with triumph. He is surrounded by William's guard but it is too late.

We carry my husband to a nearby couch and he rasps his final breaths. I lean close to him as he commends his soul and his people to God. And then he is gone. It has all happened so fast. I kneel at his side and I am numb, but not so numb that I do not instinctively reach out to God.

I feel a familiar pain in my chest again. Sharp and shooting, a terrible ache that radiates through my entire body. I cannot breathe. Every scar in my soul is ripped open once more and I feel as though I am lying beside William bleeding with him.

For a single crazed moment, I think that I too must die. I cannot live. Cannot live through this pain, this loss again. *Oh God!* I cry in silent desperation. *What will anchor me?* And then as though I am being gently pulled back by strong hands, I think of two words: consider Him. Consider Jesus who suffered. Consider Him.

It is not a moment of clarity. I am not capable of clear thought right now, but it is a moment of hope. It is as though God would have me remember that I am not alone. That the everlasting arms are beneath me. That every scar upon my soul is not foreign to Him. He knows what it is like to lose those He loves, He knows what it is like to be separated from those dear to His heart. He knows my pain. And that is enough to brace me for whatever else may come.

Louise de Coligny (1555–1620) was the daughter of the famous Huguenot general Admiral Gaspard de Coligny and granddaughter of Louise de Montmorency, chief lady-in-waiting to Margaret of Navarre. After the death of her second husband, William of Orange, Louise assumed guardianship for most of William's sixteen children. She herself had only one son, Frederick Henry, who later became Prince of Orange. She was a strong proponent of the Dutch Reformation and contributed greatly to the growth of the Reformation in the Low Countries.

5

Charlotte Duplessis de Mornay
BEAUTY FOR ASHES

Saumur, France
Summer, 1593

My dreams are filled with the sound of bells. They are the bells for Lauds, summoning the people of Paris to mass. I see the king, walking up the steps of the Cathedral of St Denis, trailed by his retinue. It is a hot day and the air is humid. I follow the king into the cool, dark confines of the cathedral and I smell the incense, bittersweet, wafting around me in a cloud. I see the monstrance and the rood, the altar and the faces of saints peering down at me. Suddenly, I want to turn and run, but my feet are stuck fast to the stone floor. I watch as the king makes his way down the nave to the altar and I am dragged along with him, as though he and I are inextricably linked, as though his choices somehow affect mine. I do not want to be here. Frantically, I try to get away but I cannot, I cannot move. I open my mouth to cry out but there is no sound. *I must get away*, I think, tugging at my feet. *I must get away. I must!* The dream, so vivid and haunting, awakens me.

I fling back the covers and stumble out of my bed. The pale moon is framed in the open window, clear and luminous in the inky sky.

A warm breeze rustles the draperies and I breathe deeply, taking a moment to calm my racing heart. There are no bells tolling around me. It has only been a dream, but at the same time it is more than a dream. It is a memory that haunts my sleep as I am sure it haunts my husband's. The events of July 25, 1593 are emblazoned in my mind, like another Parisian summer day twenty years earlier, which was also filled with the sound of bells. And yet the St Bartholomew's Day massacre did not bite into my soul as sharply as this recent betrayal.

Glancing towards our large canopied bed, I realise that I am alone in our room. I move towards the door of our privy chamber and push out into the presence chamber beyond. A single square candle burns in a window embrasure and I see Philip's form curled on the window seat, peering out into the night.

"Can you not sleep?" I ask him, my voice barely above a whisper.

He looks up then and smiles, holding out his hand to me. I go to him and twine my fingers through his, looking into his face. "Can *you* not sleep?" he asks, turning my question back on me. I shake my head.

I take a seat opposite him and tuck my feet up underneath me on the window seat, tugging my braid over my shoulder. I lean back against the cool stone wall behind me.

"I can hear the bells in my sleep. Henry's bells, the bells of St Denis," I say, staring out through the mullioned windows where the moonlight is reflected, hazy and pale.

Philip nods, gives my hand a little squeeze and then releases it. "I can hear them in my sleep as well," he says. "Only they sound like roosters crowing in the night—once, twice, three times. And I hear Henry's voice over and over again, like the voice of St Peter denying our Lord."

I smile at this and shake my head. "You have vivid dreams, my love."

"I have an overactive imagination," he says with a wry smile.

"Though perhaps you should have dreamed of Judas instead of Peter," I say, a bitter edge creeping into my voice. "For that is what Henry has done. He has not denied us, he has sold us, and very cheaply at that." Philip is quiet. What Henry has done has left a deep wound in his heart.

"You did not tell me what he told you and Sully that day. That last day before we left him. Before..." I pause, leaving the sentence hanging, not wanting to complete it.

Philip continues to stare out the window, then he shakes his head at the remembrance. *"Paris vaut bien une messe,"* he replies. Paris is well worth a mass.

For a moment I am too stunned to utter a single word. "He said that?" I ask, horrified.

"Yes, those were his words. As though this has all been nothing more than a game of cards. He weighed the odds and played his hand."

"And he played us all for fools," I say.

Last week the King of France sold his soul to secure his throne. At least that is how we, his Huguenot brothers and sisters, see it. Henry of Navarre was a handsome prince, rich with promise. He brought with him the grand legacy of his grandmother Queen Margaret of Navarre and his mother Queen Jeanne d'Albret of Navarre, both formidable scholarly women who loved the new reformist teachings. Like many of us did, Henry grew up in the very centre of the bloody and brutal war of religion. He understood clearly, as we all did, the sacrifices that needed to be made for the cause of reform, for the cause of truth.

Twenty years ago, Henry was married to Princess of Marguerite of France in an attempt to bring peace, but peace did not eventuate. We all had to wade through a bloody massacre before we realised that the wars of religion within France were not able to be solved by political means, with a strategic marriage. The St Bartholomew's Day massacre disabused us of that notion. It taught us that the conflict in France was rooted in a terrible hatred against reform.

Finally, four years ago, through some stroke of providence, Henry of Navarre, once only a distant cousin of the French king, found himself with the crown of France on his head. Henry's ascension to the throne was a moment of great rejoicing for Huguenots, who had suffered unspeakable horror for years and years. Never in our wildest dreams had we thought that we would have control of the throne. My husband Philip has stood beside Henry through thick and thin. In many ways they are brothers, not of blood, but of a common and unshakeable bond of faith. Or so we all thought.

Of course, there have been difficulties. When Henry took the throne, France rose up in all her Romanist glory and shrieked like a maiden scorned that she would never have a reformist king to rule over her. Even though Henry was clearly the only living heir when the king died, no Romanist in the realm was willing to accept it. With Philip and others at his side, Henry had to fight for the throne. The conflict was terrible. But even then, what he has done is inexcusable. It is unconscionable.

For when Henry realised that all he had to do to keep the throne was embrace Romanism, he decided that Paris was indeed well worth a mass. He turned his coat in the blink of an eye and we are all still reeling in shock. It is as though every shred of integrity has seeped from his bones. He has sold the truth for an earthly kingdom and cast a pall over the sacrifices of every good and true Huguenot who has gone before him, including his own mother, who chose to be estranged from her husband rather than recant her faith. Not one of us suspected that Henry was capable of such duplicity and such weakness.

Henry went down for a mass and they rang the bells to signal to Paris that France now had a Romanist king. These are the bells that haunt us, for we heard them tolling as we fled the city. Now the man who was once leader of the Huguenots is Catholic, and France, though wary, is reconciled to her new king.

"What will you do now?" I ask Philip, for we have only recently returned home from court.

"Stay in Saumur and lick my wounds, I suppose," he says.

"Philip..." I say, reaching out to squeeze his hand. I cannot bear to see him defeated and cowed like this. He has bent every fibre of his brilliant mind towards seeing the truth prosper in this realm and to then have it all come to this. It is like a physical blow, one far more devastating than any wound inflicted on a battlefield.

"What will *you* do?" he asks me, and I smile, trying to lighten the moment.

"Well," I say. "I am wife to the governor of Saumur, one of the strongest Huguenot provinces in France." I look at him, hoping my teasing tone will bring a smile to his lips and I am rewarded with a faint grin. "I believe I shall go about my wifely duties, the chief of which is to write a biography of my brilliant and brave husband's life."

He laughs at that. "And what, pray tell, Madame de Mornay," he says playfully, "will this biography include?"

"That, lord husband, is for me to know and for you to find out," I tease.

He shakes his head after a moment. "Are you serious?" he asks.

"I am," I say. "I want to write my account of the St Bartholomew's Day massacre too. When we came home last week and I saw the children, especially our young Philip, I realised that they need to know what we have been through. Especially since Philip is going away to Holland in a year or two. He needs to understand the history of our people. What we have fought for, what we have lost."

Philip nods slowly. He breathes a deep sigh and looks at me, his face worn, deep lines etched around his eyes and mouth. "I pray that I have been faithful, Charlotte." He pauses and I see tears shining in his eyes. "I pray that our children follow Christ with integrity all their days."

"Oh, Philip," I say, my own eyes welling with tears. "You have. Take comfort my love. You truly have."

The next day, I sit down at my desk, pull out a fresh sheet of parchment and sharpen my quill. Then I dip it in my well of ink and I begin to write.

Paris, France
August 24, 1572

The day before the massacre is like any other. Before I go to bed, I ask my lady's maid to lay out my finest clothes, for I am to pay a call at the Palace of the Louvre the next day. Then I tuck my little Susanne into bed and go to bed myself. But sometime in the night,

I am wrenched from my sleep by loud bangs, shrill screams and the insistent tolling of bells. It is a tocsin, an alarm. I tear the covers away and jump out of bed, stumbling to the windows to see what is wrong. I pull aside the curtains and push the shutters wide open. A gust of warm air strikes my face, heavy with the smells of a Parisian summer night. I lean out of the window, looking out into the street below me, the wretched bells louder now in my ears.

The moon drenches the city in its cool light. In the distance, I can see torches, winking and bobbing. Straining my ears, I think I hear chanting, rhythmic chanting, keeping time to the tolling of the tocsin. Then I hear desperate screams again. I shiver at the sounds, my mind whirling, as I try to think what could be going on outside.

I dash into the hallway outside my bedroom and immediately I see lights downstairs. The servants have heard the racket and are awake. *Thank God*, I think. I hurry downstairs and order my men to make sure that the house is secure. No-one is to leave the house, I command. We are to stay inside till daybreak and pray that whatever madness is afoot in the city will have died down by then.

Once I am sure that the house is secure, I run upstairs to the nursery. The nurse is wide-eyed with terror, sitting on the edge of her bed when I go in. I press my finger to my lips and shake my head, quietly ordering her not to make a sound. I bend over the sleeping form of my little daughter, my Susanne. She is asleep, her lips slightly parted, her hair tumbled across the pillow. I gently place my hand against her warm cheek, offering a quick prayer for her safety.

Then I slip back to my own room. I cannot sleep. I do not think any of the household will sleep. We will all sit still like the gargoyles on the walls of Notre Dame, watching and wondering what is happening in the city, praying that whatever strange, destructive force is in action will pass over us and spare us its horror. Restless, I lay down on the big bed, listening to the sounds that drift in through the window. As I listen, memories that I have kept buried rush up to meet me. They are all of my husband Jean.

I remember how he looked as he prepared to leave me to go to war. Standing in the circle of his arms, my great pregnant belly wedged between us, I wanted to plead with him to stay, but I knew better. As though he could read my mind, he gently took my face between his hands and smiled at me.

"I must go, Charlotte," he said to me. "I must do this." I remember looking into his eyes, seeing the determination there and feeling my heart sink. It was no use asking him to stay. Asking him to think about our unborn child, to think about me, his nineteen-year-old wife. "I will pray for you" is all I could say.

He nodded. "I want my son to know what it means to be a man of valour, a man of God," he said to me, his hand resting against my rounded belly. "One day, he will walk in my footsteps and I want those footsteps to lead him in the ways of God." I was silent. I knew then as I know now that this is where our convictions would take us: a fight for freedom and a martyr's end. My husband, the husbands of so many other young Huguenot girls like me, would be the casualties of this war and in that moment, staring into his eyes, I understood why they all had to fight. It was worth it, to uphold God's Word.

We were—and still are—fighting for our right to worship God according to our conscience, for our right to read the Bible in French, for our right to do away with Romanist traditions imposed upon us by the church. I understood that my husband could not be compelled to stay at home, safe with me, while his brothers in arms went to battle for their faith. He must go. It was not a war of their choosing, but it was a war they could not shrink from.

I shiver and I wonder if this is another night of war. I think of my daughter, asleep in her little bed, and I remember the night she was born. My lady mother was in the room with me and my husband was still at war. My baby was on the way and I was terrified. When she finally came, mewling and red, she was not the boy that Jean had hoped for, but it did not matter. As I looked down at her little face, I realised that this little girl would one day walk in *my* footsteps, this little girl would one day look to *me* to show her the kind of woman she should become and I knew then that the legacy I wanted to leave her is one of faithfulness to God. Unflinching, unyielding, unapologetic. I decided then that I would raise her to fear God and not man. "Favour is deceitful, and beauty is vain: but a woman that feareth the Lord, she shall be praised."

When Jean was killed and they brought me news of his death, I thought I would collapse, thought I would die. Can you die of a broken heart? I thought that I could at that moment. But I could not allow myself the luxury of falling to the ground weeping, for I was holding my five-month-old daughter in my arms. So I stood and wept for both of us. For the husband I had lost and the father she would never know. Even though my heart was breaking, I knew I must keep standing. For her sake, I must remain on my feet. For I knew that I had to raise her to be what she was born to be: a Huguenot woman, strong, brave and true. And above all dauntless in the face of fear.

I must have slept, for when I open my eyes I see that dawn is beginning to peep over the horizon, quietly lifting its pale pink head to see if it is safe to usher in the day. But it isn't, I realise, jolting upright. It isn't safe. The tocsin is still ringing and screams still thicken the morning air.

I rise from my bed and dress, then I go downstairs preparing to send one of my men to my lady mother's house not far away. I have just reached the bottom step when a scullery maid comes running down the hallway, her eyes wide with terror.

"What is it?" I ask, grabbing her shoulders. She opens her mouth like a fish and closes it again. "What has happened?" I demand.

"Oh madame! Oh madame!" she whimpers, tears shining in her eyes. "They are killing everyone!"

"Killing?" I breathe, and she nods sobbing.

"They are killing all those of our religion. They are killing Huguenots."

"Where?" I ask, and then unable to bear it any longer I give her a little shake. "Tell me, Idette! Where?"

She sucks in a deep shuddering breath and looks me in the eye. "All through the city," she says, her voice wobbly. "They say that all through Paris the streets are running red with blood." She covers her face with her hands and begins to sob.

I leave her and run down the hall to the windows in the foyer that face the street. I peer outside and my blood runs cold. There, at the far end of the Rue de Antoine where I am staying, is a column of guards. Even at this distance, I can see white crosses painted across the front of their helmets. *Distinguishing them, no doubt*, I think in terror. *Setting them apart. Separating the Catholics from the Huguenots.*

I force myself into action once more and run back to the kitchen. I immediately dispatch one of my men to go to my mother and then to my uncle. Surely they will know what I must do? They are Catholic and my uncle is a bishop, but surely they will protect me? For what other crime have I committed than being a Huguenot?

Finally, after half an hour of waiting and watching the madness on the street worsen, I make up my mind. I go upstairs and bundle Susanne in her clothes, then I place her in the hands of my most trusted servant and send her to one of our close friends. He is the master in the king's household and he is sure to keep her safe. After they have left, I go to the small chapel at the back of the house and I get down on my knees and pray: "He that dwelleth in the secret place of the most High"...I hear shouts outside, men's voices colliding with piercing screams..."shall abide under the shadow of the Almighty"...Is Susanne alright? Have they made it safely to Monsieur de Perreuze's home? "I will say of the Lord, He is my refuge and my fortress: my God; in him will I trust."

"Madame," the soft voice rouses me, and I jump to my feet, turning to face the servant.

"Is she alright?" I ask, my voice trembling. "Did you take her to Monsieur de Perreuze?"

He nods. "Monsieur de Perreuze sent a message. He says that you too can come to his house if you are in need of a safe place to stay."

I pause, my mind keeping pace with my racing heart, as I consider this offer. Finally I nod. "Yes," I say. "Yes, I will go."

I leave with nothing but the clothes on my back. There is no time to pack and anything I take would only slow me down and make me look suspicious. As I am slipping out the back door, I hear a thudding on the front door. The servant hurries me out into the street and I pull the hood of my cloak over my head. We hurry down the Rue de Antoine, my head low. At the end of the narrow, cobbled road I toss a glance over my shoulder and see men beating down my front door.

"They are servants of the Duke of Guise," my servant murmurs. "They are searching for all known Huguenots. Your late husband fought with the Admiral, madame. They know you. They know where you live."

I look up at him and fear engulfs me once more. "The Admiral," I ask. "Is he..." It is a question that I cannot finish, and the man's eyes glaze over for a moment before he shakes his head and looks away.

When I reach the home of Monsieur de Perreuze, I am trembling like a leaf. The horrors I have seen on the short walk here are seared into my mind and I do not think I shall ever forget them. I have never seen so much blood, never seen so much hatred. The servants lead me into Monsieur de Perreuze's library. They bring me bread and press a mug into my hands.

"Ah, Charlotte," Monsieur de Perreuze's quiet voice brings my head up. I rise to my feet, lay the mug aside and go to him. He gathers me close in a fatherly embrace and I think of how much I miss my father.

"What is happening, monsieur?" I ask as I pull away.

He motions for me to take a seat and lowers himself into a vacant chair opposite me. He sighs. "They have killed the Admiral," he says, and I feel my eyes water.

"Admiral de Coligny?" I ask, as though there were any other admiral in France. He nods. I bow my head and squeeze my eyes shut. "He...my late husband...my Jean loved him very much," I whisper. I look up and the compassion in de Perreuze's eyes warms me.

"He was a good man," Monsieur de Perreuze says. "It is a senseless death and France is poorer for it."

"Who...who ordered this? Why is this happening?" I ask.

He is silent for a moment, studying me. Finally, he says, "They say the king gave the order."

"The king?" I cannot fathom it. "Why?"

Monsieur de Perreuze shrugs. "It was politically expedient. I do not know, Charlotte. No-one knows what has possessed the king to sanction this madness. To think that only a week ago he was giving his sister in marriage to Henry of Navarre, the most powerful Huguenot in the realm. And now this."

"Is…Where is the King of Navarre now?" I ask. *Surely the king is not so mad as to kill his own brother-in-law?* I wonder.

"I hear he is safe for now. But you are not, Charlotte. No Huguenot is. They will kill you if they find out who you are."

Monsieur de Perreuze begins to paint a picture of what has transpired. He tells me that no Huguenot has been spared. Nobles who have been the king's guests at the Palace of the Louvre have been dragged out of their beds and butchered in the galleries. Streets have been scoured, doors banged upon, and every Huguenot who has been found has been killed in the street. "They say the Seine is filled with bodies," he says, his voice trembling. "They say it runs red, like a river of blood." I cannot take it in. I cannot grasp it.

Monsieur de Perreuze tells me that I am not the only Huguenot seeking refuge inside his home. He is a Catholic and yet he is harbouring Huguenots. If he is discovered, they will kill him as surely as they will kill us. *Not all Catholics are heretics and not all Huguenots are saints*, I think to myself. *Only God reads the thoughts of the heart.*

August 27, 1572

We stay at the de Perreuze home for three days, huddled in the attic, jumping at every sound we hear. I cannot sleep and my food tastes like sandpaper, but I eat mechanically, forcing myself to chew and swallow to keep up my strength for my girl. Then our worst fears materialise. The de Perreuze family comes under suspicion and they are told that their house will be searched for Huguenots.

"I am so sorry, Charlotte. It is a dreadful position to be in, for us both," Monsieur de Perreuze says, taking my hand and patting it absently. He is too preoccupied to give me his full attention. After all, what will happen to him if he is found harbouring Huguenots? The Duke of Guise will not spare him, that is for sure. I smile sympathetically at him and squeeze his hand.

"You have been so kind to us, monsieur," I say softly, assuming that means to turn us out of his home. I can not hold it against him. "Even though we differ in our religious persuasions, you have offered me and mine a place of refuge and I will always be grateful to you for your kindness."

"Ah, child." His eyes finally find mine and he smiles gently. "Your father and I were friends for many years and I have known you since you were a wee babe, just like your Susanne. I cannot turn you over to that ravenous mob, no matter what you believe. It would be too cruel to even contemplate. Now come, we must make plans." When I hear these words, I am weak with relief and gratitude. This dear, kind man will not turn me out, even if it means risking his own life.

When the soldiers come, I am crammed into a hollow gable perched high in the house. Along with the tramp of feet echoing through the eerily hushed rooms, I hear the screams of the dying outside. It has been three long days and yet the killing continues. It is such a frenzied, interminable massacre that no-one can believe it. I fear that the screams of the dying will be forever etched in my mind, that I will never be able to rid myself of this horror, no matter how hard I try.

Hiding in the gable, behind a false wall, I shudder as the wails pierce the space around me. My hands are clasped tightly in my lap and there is an ache in my jaw. I realise my teeth are clamped down tight and I am trembling. Fear rolls over me in waves. I have left Susanne downstairs in another hiding spot with her nurse and I am terrified that they will find her. For one terror-stricken moment, I imagine my child being torn apart by the mob. I contemplate flinging myself down from the roof, for it would be better to die than to witness that or to be captured by the mob myself. But in that moment of confused grief, I turn to God.

There, in that hollow spot, I bring to mind every psalm that I have learned. Over and over I repeat the words, for what do I have left to cling to? Only the arm of God. Only the Word of God. I have nothing else. Nothing. My husband is dead. I have nothing but the clothes on my back to call my own, and my precious daughter and I are at this very moment at risk of our lives. And for what? Because I refuse to bow down to the host at mass, because I read the Bible in French, because I refuse to surrender the freedom of my conscience.

"I will lift up mine eyes unto the hills," I whisper, rocking myself back and forth in my little prison. I hear the tramp of soldiers' feet climbing the stairs. "From whence cometh my help?" A door crashes open and I hear footfalls. I rock harder, biting into the soft inner flesh of my cheek, frantically repeating the psalm in my mind: "My help cometh from the Lord, which made heaven and earth. He will not suffer thy foot to be moved. He that keepeth thee will not slumber."

The footsteps recede and I am safe. Safe for the moment. But I still hear screams below and I know that my safety is as fragile as a silk thread.

When I make my way downstairs, I find that they have sent Susanne to my grandmother. Her nurse bundled her tightly against her chest and walked quietly through the braying and bloody throng. We receive word later that she is safe. My lady grandmother is Catholic and she is also of noble birth. I am torn when I hear that Susanne has been sent there. Part of me is glad that she is safe, but another part of me wonders at what cost? Will Jean and I wade through blood for our faith only to have our daughter raised a Romanist? And yet I cannot linger upon these thoughts for long. The intensity of the struggle around me is enough for me to bear without adding to the burden. At least, I think, a little part of Jean and I will survive this massacre even if I do not.

As the day wears on, we hear of more deaths, even deaths of high parliamentary officials close to the king. It seems that no Huguenot is safe, no matter their proximity to the throne. We begin to realise that we cannot stay any longer at the de Perreuze home, for doing so would jeopardise our own lives and the lives of our hosts.

I try to go to my lady mother but they have stationed guards at her home in case I try to come to her. Finally, in desperation, I make my way to the home of one of my mother's maids. Her husband, a blacksmith, is one of the leaders of the uprising in this quarter. But my lady mother sends word to assure me that the chambermaid and her husband will shelter me. The irony is not wasted on me. While the blacksmith is out massacring other Huguenots like me, I am being sheltered under his roof and fed at his table. I am grateful to have survived yet another day of this horror. I do not stay with the blacksmith and his chambermaid wife for long. From there, I am moved from one house to another, always travelling in the dead of night, shrunk into my cloak, as I weave my way through the frenzied mob.

August 31, 1572

Finally, after more than a week of this massacre, my lady mother gathers her courage and comes to me. She tries to convince me that I must attend mass to save my life but I refuse.

"Think of the child," she tells me, wringing her hands.

"I am," I tell her. I clasp her hands in mine, my eyes searching her face, willing her to understand my convictions. "I am thinking of Susanne."

Tears form in her eyes. "Stop this," she tells me in a trembling voice. "Stop this foolishness and come to mass. We will go together and you will kneel before the altar and bow down to the host and it will be alright. You will see. It will all be over and you can put this behind you once and for all."

I grip her hands more tightly. "Lady mother, I can't. Don't you see? I can't do it."

"One mass," she pleads. "Just one mass to save your life. Or if you care nothing for yourself, then at the very least to save the life of your child."

I shake my head. "I can't, Mama." I struggle for a moment, trying to find the right words to help her understand. "How can I turn my back on God when He has been so faithful, so good to me?" I finally say softly.

She shakes her head impatiently, her eyes clouding with anger. "How could you possibly be turning your back on God by going to mass?" she snaps. "Do you think that I have turned my back on God because I go to mass?"

"It is idolatry," I say, my eyes filling with tears at the pain I know I am causing her. I love my mother, but I can't allow that to cloud my faith.

"So you say," she tells me, with a hard edge to her voice.

"I do not believe that a handful of Latin words spoken over a wafer transform it into the literal body of Christ. The Bible doesn't speak of mass the way it is celebrated by the church, lady mother. The Bible doesn't speak of purgatory or penance either."

"You're being a fool," she says angrily. "A stubborn young fool. I will not stand by and watch you hacked to pieces for it. Do you hear me, Charlotte? I will not stand by and watch it!" She pauses her tirade to take a breath. "We cannot keep Susanne," she says abruptly. "You will have to take her."

I stare at her unblinkingly for a moment and then I realise that she is using Susanne to try to force my hand. I shake my head. "Then let me have her. I will take her with me and we will leave Paris in search of refuge."

"Leave Paris?" she scoffs. "Do you know that every gate is shut? The river is so full of bodies that it looks like a single mass of floating humanity. And the stench! The entire city reeks of rotting flesh and death. They will recognise you as a Huguenot the moment you step out of this house and kill you both."

"Then I will take my chances," I reply, my chin tipped resolutely. "I will not attend mass," I tell her softly but in a tone of unmistakable finality.

"You are being a fool," she says again, but this time I can see in her eyes that her heart is breaking. "Even if you don't believe in it anymore, what harm will it do you to simply go through the motions to save your life? To save the life of your child?" We stare each other down for a long and tenuous moment. *"Ta vie vaut bien une messe,"* she says.

"Mama," I begin softly, my own heart breaking as I take in the agony on her face. "My life may well be worth a mass, but my faith is not." I gently wipe a tear from her cheek. "If you are free to believe that the host is the very body of Christ, then why can I not be free to deny it? If you are free to follow popes and councils, why can I not be free to follow the Word of God alone?"

I kiss her cold fingers and take a small step away from her. "Lady mother, neither you, nor the king, nor the mob who calls for my blood can force me to violate my conscience. My faith is not worth a mass. I will not sacrifice my faith in God's Word for anything."

Escape from Paris
September, 1572

I decide that I can no longer stay in Paris. It is a risk to leave but I begin to realise that it is a greater risk to stay. We had all thought that the massacre would last no more than a few days, but it has been more than a week and I fear that, if I do not leave, I will be butchered like the rest. I quietly make arrangements to take passage on a boat leaving the city. I am taking a long route but I have little choice. My safest option is to go by river and I have decided that I will go as far as Sens and then go overland to Epernay to my brother's estate and from there on to Sedan.

Dressed as a chambermaid, I am brought down to the quay by a servant. The sky is just lightening and the river looks sluggish and grey in the pale dawn. I huddle on the landing waiting for the boat and when it finally pulls alongside us, I see that it is a small vessel. I climb on board and find myself seated on the hard deck with seven other passengers: two monks, a priest and two merchants with their wives. They all watch me with suspicion. Why would a young unmarried woman be travelling alone at this hour of the morning? I keep my eyes low and my head tucked into my hood. I am praying, constantly praying, as the boat bobs and weaves down the river. Remembering the reports of bodies in the water, I dare not look over the side for fear that I might see someone I know.

We reach Thomery, a small village along the Seine, and I am beginning to drift off to sleep, pleasantly warmed by the morning sunshine, when the boat pulls alongside a little landing and we are boarded. I jolt awake and stare at the formidable figures of a small company of guards. Their eyes dart around the little vessel and they take us all in.

"Passports," one of them says gruffly.

I feel the icy prickle of dread tingle down my spine. I am travelling without papers, without any identification. I stare at them wide-eyed as they make their way towards me, and they immediately see my fear.

"Passport, mademoiselle," one of the guards says to me.

I open my mouth but no sound comes out. "I . . . I forgot," I finally say lamely.

The man's eyes narrow and he steps forward, grabs me roughly by the arm and hauls me to my feet. At that moment I realise how alone I am. My father is dead, my husband is dead and my brothers are like me, fugitives on the run. I tremble as I stare into the man's flinty eyes.

"You forgot?" he mocks. "How convenient. I suppose you have also forgotten your name?"

"Charlotte," I say quickly. "Charlotte . . ." I hesitate a moment, wondering if I should use Jean's last name or my own. Which is more dangerous? Which is more widely known as being Huguenot. "Charlotte Arbaleste de la Borde," I finally say, rapping out my own name.

"And are you a Huguenot, Mademoiselle de la Borde?"

Every eye on the boat is watching me. "I . . ." I stutter, and the guard tightens his grip on my arm, twisting painfully. I am terrified. What if they kill me? What if they kill me right here on this deck and then throw my body overboard? Am I ready to die? Oh God, am I ready to die?

"She's a Huguenot!" The accusing voice of the guard holding me cuts through my fog of fear. He shakes me like a rat.

"Throw her into the river," another guard says. "Make sure she drowns."

"Please." I find my voice and swallow back a sob. I cannot fall apart now. I need to hold myself together and get out of this mess.

"Please?" The guard squeezes my arm again and begins to haul me to the edge of the boat. I stumble and bang my knee hard. Another guard comes to help, grabbing my free arm, and between them they haul me up onto the side of the vessel.

"Wait!" I say, as they prepare to throw me over. "Wait! Someone can vouch for me. Monsieur Voysenon. He lives here in Thomery. He is an accountant, an auditor. He handles my lady grandmother's estate and is a strong Roman Catholic. He can vouch for me."

The guards pause and consider what I have said for a moment. "Please," I beg. "Please. I can give you the directions. Take me to him and I promise you he will vouch for me...that...that my family is Catholic." I close my eyes briefly, praying that they do not question me more closely. "Please."

Perhaps it is because I look so young or perhaps it is because I am so pale with terror, but the guards relent and take me to Monsieur Voysenon. When I get to the house, a servant opens the gate and goes pale at the sight of the guards. I speak to him rapidly, telling him that I am a friend of Monsieur Voysenon and that I must see him at once. The man opens the gate for us and I leave the guards in the courtyard outside while I hurry inside, praying that they will not follow me. The servant takes me to Monsieur Voyenson, who is startled to see me and in such a state of fear.

"Why have you come?" he asks me, lightly grabbing my arm and leading me away from his milling manservant.

"I am in trouble," I tell him, my voice barely above a whisper. I quickly explain my situation to him and he shakes his head.

"Ah child," he says. "Do you know how many Huguenots I have sheltered during this madness? Too many to count."

"Will you help me, monsieur?" I ask him, my voice edged with desperation. "If you do not vouch for me, they will drown me. Please. It seems that God has made you the only means of saving my life."

He sighs and nods. "Come," he says. "Let me speak to them." We find them in the kitchens, where the cook has been only too glad to oblige them with some bread and drink, especially given the size of their swords.

"I trust you have been well taken care of, monsieurs." Monsieur Voyenson is all smiles and jovial hospitality. The men nod and stand from their places at the rough table. They tower over poor Monsieur Voyenson and I see him swallow hard as he looks up at them, his adam's apple bobbing up and down in his slender throat.

"You know Mademoiselle de la Borde?" one of the guards asks without preamble.

Monsieur Voyenson nods. "Yes," he says. Then he tips his head to the side, eyeing the guards. "I am a Catholic myself and I have known Mademoiselle de la Borde's family a long time. Her grandmother is a devoted Romanist and her uncle is a bishop of the church. I see no reason to suspect this family of reformed leanings."

"We are not questioning the faith of the mademoiselle's family," the guard says gruffly. "We are questioning the faith of the mademoiselle herself." He flicks a glance at me and my mouth goes dry. What will Monsieur Voyenson say? He cannot lie. Surely I cannot expect him to lie. Silently, I offer a desperate prayer for deliverance.

At that moment, Madame Voyenson strolls into the kitchen, smiling benignly. "I heard we had visitors," she says. The guards give her a cursory nod and then she looks over at me. "Ah Charlotte. I had not heard that you were with us."

She comes and wraps me in a warm embrace. It is like a little slice of heaven and my legs nearly buckle under me, I am so weary and terrified. She holds me up and then leans back, looking into my eyes. She then turns to face the guards. "And what will you do with the young mademoiselle?" she asks.

"By God," one of them responds, "if we find her to be a Huguenot, we will take her to the river and drown her." My knees go limp beneath me, forcing me to ease myself down onto a nearby bench.

Madame Voyenson shakes her head. "I am a Catholic. I attend mass every day, and yet with all this madness around me, I have been

116

in such a state of fear that I have had a fever for a week." She shakes her head. "It is a sad business," she says softly. I press my hand to my chest, as though I am attempting to keep my heart from flying out of it.

The guards shuffle and then one of them says, "I know what that fear is like, madame. I too have been terrified since the massacre began."

"It is a terrible thing," she says softly, "that we inflict such pain on our own countrymen. Were we in their place, I am sure we would crave some measure of mercy."

The air is thick with tension for a long moment and then, as if by some miracle of grace, the men's faces soften. They nod, haul me to my feet, gently this time, and take me back to the boat where they allow me to continue my journey in peace. I am in such a state of shock that it is not until I have reached Sens and disembarked from the boat that I am able to process what has happened. And then I can only fall on my knees and give thanks to God. I am alive and it is only by His mercy.

I have made it out of Paris alive, but my journey is far from over. I know that I must make it to Sedan if I am to be safe. Sedan is the Huguenot stronghold where I was sheltered when Jean was at war and I was pregnant with Susanne.

I have joined the rest of the group I travelled with, the priest and the monks and the merchants and their wives, at an inn for the night. Their conversation revolves around the massacre and they express such delight in the killing of Huguenots that I have to bite my tongue to keep my retorts at bay. Finally, when I can bear it no more, I rise from the table, excuse myself and make my way to my room. I am disgusted but I also need to plan.

On the way to my room, I am stopped by a man. He is dressed in travel-stained clothes and his face is hidden under a dark hood. At first I rear back in fear, but then he pushes the hood back and in the flickering torch light I recognise him. "Menier!" I gasp. I am overcome by a sudden urge to run into his arms and hug him. He is my lady grandmother's manservant.

Quietly, he pulls me into the shadows along the wall and gives a small bow. "Madame," he says softly, "your lady grandmother sent me. She got word that you were going to Sens and she sent me to make sure you are alright." His eyes scan my face. "You are well?"

I nod, biting down on my trembling lip, as I think about my close call at Thomery. "Menier, I am on my way to Sedan," I say. "I can take refuge with the Duke and Duchess of Bouillon there. I had planned to break my journey in Epernay at my brother's estate. Will you accompany me?"

He is quiet for a moment and then he nods. "I will accompany you," he says. He thinks for a moment and then adds, "We can pass as a merchant and his sister for the time being. Have you any money?"

I nod. "Yes, I have some money but I am running low and we will need at least a donkey to make the journey to Sedan."

"Your lady grandmother sent you some money. I have it with me and it will be enough to secure horses and rooms to get us to your brother." I am so overwhelmed with gratitude when I hear of my grandmother's generosity that I do not trust myself to speak. "Meet me outside in the courtyard at dawn," he whispers. "We will mingle with the crowd and get away from your travelling company. After that, we will find our way to your brother and then on to Sedan."

I nod, tears creeping into my eyes. His appearance is an answer to my prayers and I reach out and squeeze his arm. "Thank you, Menier," I say in a choked voice. "God sent you to take me the rest of the way."

His eyes soften in the dim light. "God will not fail you, Charlotte," he says softly. "He will get you to Sedan safely, I am certain of that."

I reach my brother's chateau in Epernay with relative ease. My grandmother's funds go a long way towards securing us sturdy horses and simple lodgings along the way. When we ride into the courtyard at my brother's home and call for grooms, the shadows are lengthening across the sky and the sun is sinking low. At first no-one recognises me, but when I pull off my cloak, there are gasps of recognition and someone goes to find my brother. Another servant leads me into the great hall, where I sink exhausted into a chair.

"Sister!"

I jump and turn around, and the tears that I have held back for so long gather and spill over my cheeks. "Oh, Pierre," I murmur, as I fall into his arms. He hugs me tight and is quiet while I sob into his shoulder.

"It's alright," he says softly. "You are safe here. Everything will be alright, you will see."

I pull back and look into his face "What news? Have you heard from Mama?" He nods thoughtfully and leads me back to the chair. He sits next to me and sees that I am trembling.

"You are cold!" he exclaims. He calls for a hot drink and before long a servant appears with a big mug and a red hot poker. Carefully, he hands me the mug and then plunges the poker into it. The drink seethes and bubbles, a spicy smell wafting around me like a blanket. When the bubbling begins to peter out, he withdraws the poker and leaves the room. I wrap my hands around the mug and sip, closing my eyes as I swallow.

"Did you come alone?" Pierre asks.

I open my eyes. "No," I say. "Grandmama sent Menier to Sens to meet me. She had heard that I was going there."

Pierre nods slowly. "You had no trouble on the road?"

I bite my lip. "Some," I say and then tell him of the close shave in Thomery.

He sucks in a sharp breath and shakes his head. "God be praised that you are safe," he murmurs and I nod.

I study him, taking in the strong, familiar planes of his face. "Where are Claudette and the children?" I ask.

"I have sent them to the house in Eprunes, on Grandmama's estate. I think it is safer there."

"Are they safe? Have you been in danger here?" I ask.

He looks at me then, his eyes locking onto mine and a flicker of something passes across his face.

"You must be tired," he says, and I nod, taking another long sip of the drink. "Come, let us get you something to eat and settle you in for the night. Tomorrow morning, we can go to chapel together and then discuss further plans."

"Yes" I agree, my stomach growling at the thought of a good meal. "And I could use a bath."

Pierre chuckles. "That can be arranged. I will have some of the servants draw one for you."

Later, as I step into the large wooden tub of hot water, I feel as though I am in heaven. I haven't had a bath in so long and I am so grateful for small mercies. They have added something to the water, lavender perhaps? It smells so good, I feel like I might soak in it all night. When the water is finally tepid and I have scrubbed myself clean, I step out and get dressed for the night. It is only when I am drifting off to sleep in the big comfortable bed that I realise that my brother never answered my questions.

The next morning, I awake once more to the ringing of bells and it takes me a moment to orient myself. Then I realise that they are the bells for Prime and I frown. Why would Pierre be ringing bells for morning mass? I rise, get dressed and go downstairs.

As I reach the walkway leading down to the chapel, I see my brother ahead of me and I hurry to meet him, the soles of my soft leather shoes tapping against the pathway. "Pierre!" I call.

He hears me and turns to wait for me. "How was your bath?" he asks grinning, when I have caught up to him. I take the arm he offers me and smile.

"Heavenly," I reply and he chuckles.

"Did you sleep well?" he asks.

"Yes," I nod. "It was so nice to finally sleep in a good, soft bed."

"Well, I am glad," he says, patting my hand. "Have you thought of what you will do next?" he asks. "You told me you wanted to go to Sedan?"

I nod. "That was my plan," I say, but I am beginning to wonder if I can't just stay here with my brother. He seems to be at peace and this chateau is one we used to come to as children. It would be so nice to stay. I could even bring Susanne here and we could lay low for a while.

As if sensing my thoughts, he offers, "You are welcome to stay, Charlotte. Claudette and the children will be here in a few weeks and Susanne could join her cousins." The offer is so tempting, but we are almost to the chapel and my reply is swallowed by the hollow ringing of the bells.

"Why are you ringing bells for Prime?" I ask him suddenly, remembering the question I woke up to. He is quiet as he leads me into the chapel. Once we are through the doors, I stop short and gasp. "No!" I say, looking up at him. "What is this?"

"Charlotte." He turns to me with a frown and shakes his head as if to deter me from saying anything. I look away, blinking back tears from my eyes. At the front of the chapel is a priest standing before an altar, readying it for the mass, and there, large as life, is an ornate monstrance, holding the host. I glance at my brother in horror before turning around and walking out of the chapel.

Tears are streaming down my cheeks as the significance of what I have just witnessed washes over me. He follows me down the pathway. "Charlotte!" he calls. "Charlotte, wait!"

He grabs my arm and turns me around, but I pull away from him. "How could you?" I ask. "You are a Huguenot, Pierre!"

"I had to take a mass to save myself and my family," he says.

"Where?" I ask. "When?"

"In Paris." His voice is quiet. "At our lady mother's insistence."

"She insisted that I take a mass too but I refused her. How could you do this, Pierre? You know what the Bible says. Why would you turn your back on it like this?"

"I had no choice," he snaps angrily.

"You always have a choice!"

"It was just one mass, Charlotte," he says, turning away from me and pacing like a caged lion.

"If it was just one mass, then tell me why you are ringing bells for Prime? And why is there a priest and an altar and a monstrance inside your chapel? It is not just one mass, Pierre! You have gone back!"

He sighs heavily and turns to me. "Yes," he says after a long silence. "I have gone back. And I was hoping you would join me."

"What?" I stare at him in shock.

"Haven't you suffered enough, Charlotte? Jean is dead, you are separated from Susanne, running like an animal hunted for its life. What has this reformed faith ever given you but grief and loss?"

"It has given me peace and hope and joy. God is my refuge, my friend. I *love* Him! He has given me everything! I cannot turn my back on Him for so little when he has given me so much."

"So little? Fine clothes, a fine house, a luxurious life. These are hardly little things," Pierre glares at me.

"They are little things in comparison to everything else he has given me, Pierre. I won't turn my back on God. Not now," my voice is soft, all the fight has left me. "I must leave," I say after a long silence.

He looks at me, his eyes clouding with fear. "Where will you go?" he asks me.

"To Sedan, like I told you."

"The roads are dangerous, Charlotte. You might not make it. They are still killing and this mob makes no distinction between men, women and children."

"Then I will have to take that risk. I can't stay here, Pierre. You know I can't. I will only put you in danger and make things harder for you." I sigh and smile sadly at him. "You are my brother, my blood and I love you, but I can't walk the path you are on. It is best if we go our separate ways."

We stare at each other, neither of us willing to make the first move. I think of our childhood, here in this home and in other places. Pierre was always the instigator in our play, the rest of us tagging along behind him. I think of all my siblings at that moment, my two other brothers and my sister, all of us scattered throughout the kingdom, all of us facing our own choices and my heart squeezes painfully. Sometimes the cost of following your conscience is almost too high to count.

"I will arrange transport for you," Pierre says finally. I am about to protest but he shakes his head. "You're my sister, Charlotte. It's my duty to keep you safe."

I realise then what he has been doing. The mass was his final attempt to protect me, to be my big brother. I go to him and put my hand on his arm, my eyes meeting his with a small, sad smile. "God will keep me safe, Pierre," I say.

He arranges for a wagon to take me to Sedan, then meets me in the early hours of the next morning to say goodbye.

"Did you manage to have another bath?" he asks me, in an attempt at humour.

I smile. "I did," I say. "Though I am sure the Duchess of Bouillon will make sure I am comfortable when I get to Sedan." He nods. I step forward to embrace him and we hold each other tightly. "Goodbye, Pierre," I say softly. "God be with you."

Menier accompanies me on my journey to Sedan and it takes us nearly a week to get there. We stop at inns along the way, always careful to conceal our identities, posing as a merchant and his widowed sister. On the final day of our journey, I decide that we should push on without stopping for the night. The stories we have heard along the way scare me and I want to get to Sedan as quickly as I can.

We reach Sedan in the wee hours of the morning. Dawn is breaking over the horizon as the wagon clatters into the courtyard of the imposing chateau and Menier calls for the grooms of the stable. Men hurry outside and there is a flurry of activity around us. Every bone in my body aches from the jarring of the wagon. I am exhausted and so discouraged. I have never felt so alone in my life. My entire family is Catholic and I alone am a Huguenot. I feel homeless and adrift.

When I step out of the wagon, I stumble and nearly fall. I feel a strong hand around my arm, steadying me. "Are you alright?"

I look up and find myself staring into a pair of golden-brown eyes. "Yes," I say, attempting a smile. "I am alright." I straighten myself and take a better look at the man in front of me. "I am Charlotte Arbaleste de la Borde," I say by way of introduction.

He takes the hand I offer him and sweeps a bow. "Yes, we have been expecting you, Madame de la Borde. Your grandmother's servant sent word ahead, telling us that you were on your way here. The Duke and Duchess have been worried about you. Have you had a good journey?"

"As well as can be expected," I say wryly, rubbing my back.

He smiles again. "Have you travelled alone?"

I shrug and bite my lip. "Menier has travelled with me," I say gesturing to the manservant who is helping the grooms to tend to the horses. "But . . . other than that I am alone."

He tips his head, regarding me. "Not anymore," he says. "You have family here. Brothers and sisters in Christ."

I feel such an overwhelming rush of gratitude at his words that my eyes sting with tears. "Thank you," I whisper.

He shrugs. "It is the truth."

"What is your name, monsieur?" I ask.

"I am Philip," he says. "Philip Duplessis de Mornay." He offers me his arm. "Come," he says. "Let me take you to the duchess."

I take his arm and allow him to lead me towards the massive chateau, glad that I am no longer alone. Little do I realise that this is the beginning of a new chapter in my life and that this man standing beside me will offer me his arm to lean on for a long time to come.

Paris, France

Summer, 1595

I am standing at the window, watching the throng of people as they jostle each other in the streets below, my mind filled with memories of that long-ago day when I reached Sedan and first met Philip.

Looking back, I see that first meeting for what it truly was: a new beginning. God was giving me beauty for ashes. Only now do I see it clearly, all these years later.

The door opens and I turn to see my son standing in the doorway. "Lady mother, are you ready?" he asks.

I smile at him. He is so much like his father. "Yes," I reply. "I am ready."

He offers me his arm, in the same way his father does, and I take it and walk beside him. "Where are we going today, lady mother?" he asks me, as we make our way downstairs.

"I have a surprise for you," I say to him. "There is someone I would like you to meet before you leave for the Low Countries. There is also something I would like to give you."

"Who is it?" he asks with a smile. "And what is it?"

I grin at him. "You'll see."

Of all the people I had thought to meet this summer, as I prepare to bid farewell to my boy, Louise de Coligny was furthest from my mind. It has been so long since I last saw her. I had heard of her marriage to the Prince of Orange and of her subsequent widowhood, but I never expected to see her here in France.

I want Philip to meet her before he goes away. I have finished writing my book for him and even now it is tucked among my luggage at our lodgings. In it, I have chronicled that terrible massacre we all lived through. This is one of the reasons I want Philip to meet Louise. She was there that night and is a living link to the past. There is much that Philip can learn from Louise about our past, about our legacy as Huguenots.

We are ushered into a parlour in the home where the dowager princess is staying and when she sees me, she jumps to her feet and hugs me as though we were young girls again. My first husband, Jean de Pas, fought alongside Louise's father, Admiral Gaspard de Coligny, and was acquainted with her first husband, Charles de Teligny. Louise has also relied heavily on my husband Philip for counsel since her own husband, the Prince of Orange, was killed. She writes to him often and the two of us occasionally exchange letters.

Perhaps what binds us is our losses. We both lost husbands when we were still teenage girls. We both remarried strong, deeply devoted reformist men. But perhaps what builds the greatest affinity between us is the fact that we both survived the massacre. We were survivors of that great reaping of human blood and we have gone on to thrive by the grace of God.

My boy, my Philip, has heard of the princess but this is his first time meeting her. "How much like Monsieur de Mornay he looks," Louise says, as she smiles at him.

"He is our pride and joy," I tell her quietly, and she meets my eyes with a smile and a nod. We are both Huguenot mothers. We know the value of a son who is alive and has been spared the perils of war.

"And you go to Holland?" she asks Philip, as we take our seats.

"Yes, your Highness," Philip says. "I wish to study and then perhaps take up arms." Louise shoots me a startled glance.

"We have yet to fully discuss it," I say, clearing my throat. "His father and I wish him to study in Holland and after that we shall see."

Louise nods. "How is Monsieur de Mornay, Charlotte?" she asks, and I know what she means. How is my husband faring under the strain of Henry's reign?

"As well as can be expected," I reply.

"Yes…We have all learned to adapt and survive whatever is thrown our way."

"It has been a necessity for us as Huguenots," I agree.

She smiles then and looks at Philip. "I shall tell my step-son Maurice to watch over you," she says.

Maurice is Prince of Orange now and he wields considerable power. It would mean so much to me for Philip to come under the protection of such a powerful man. My eyes mist with tears and I thank her gratefully.

After some time, we finish our visit and as we rise to leave, Louise enfolds me in a long embrace. "Stay strong, my sister," she whispers in my ear. "After all that we have been through, you cannot lay down your arms now." I nod and squeeze her tight, before stepping away and walking out of the room.

The next morning, I hand Philip a small leather-bound book. "What is this?" he asks, taking it from me and flipping open the embossed cover.

"It is a biography. A retelling of your father's life and mine. Of all the perils and struggles we have encountered over the past decades."

He fingers the pages almost reverently, slowly thumbing through them, scanning the words on the thick paper. "You wrote this, lady mother?" he asks, looking up at me.

I nod and sit down on the bed next to him. "I wrote it so that you will remember who you are, Philip. So that you will never forget that you are a Huguenot. Your legacy is not war or a fine career, your legacy is faithfulness to God." I reach up and brush back a lock of his hair and smile tenderly at him. "Promise me that you will read it," I say softly.

"Every word," he promises. I lean over to hug him. He squeezes me back and then pulls away and pauses, looking down into my face. "Have you written about the massacre?" he finally asks.

I nod. Taking the book from him, I turn the pages and set the open book on his lap. "I have written an eyewitness account of what I went through at the time," I say, pointing to the page where the story starts.

"Then that is where I will begin," he says, squeezing my hand.

Charlotte Duplessis de Mornay (1548–1606) became a Protestant following the conversion of her father, the French Viscount Guy Arbaleste II, to the reformed faith. Her account of the St Bartholomew's Day massacre is one of the few surviving eyewitness accounts of the event that has come down to us today. This, along with the memoirs she wrote of both her own life and her second husband's life, are among the most significant contributions she made to the Reformation. She married Philip Duplessis de Mornay in January, 1576, and they had eight children together, five of whom died while they were still in infancy. Her son Philip, to whom she dedicated the memoir of her husband's life, died in 1605 fighting alongside the Dutch. Heartbroken over his death, Charlotte died a few months later in May, 1606.

6

Marie Durand

IN THE SHADOW OF THE SWORD

Aigues-Mortes, France

Spring, 1745

I am drowning. I wake up with my face pressed against the cold stone floor, water swirling around me. I gasp and take in a mouthful of putrid, foul-tasting water. Sputtering, I sit up, struggling to catch my breath. It is dark. So dark that I cannot see my hand in front of my face. All I can feel is water, seeping into my clothes, cold and slimy with refuse. Shuddering, I struggle to my feet. The water is almost to my ankles.

Around me, I hear gasps and murmurs as the other women struggle awake, experiencing the same rude shock that I have. I hear the gush of water and I realise that it is raining heavily outside. The Tower of Constance, where we are held, is a circular tower built of stone. There is a hole in the roof that lets in a small shaft of sunlight during the day. It also lets in rain, hail, sleet and snow. There is a similar hole in the floor which is for our refuse. Tonight, it has obviously been unable to cope with the downpour flooding in through the roof and the water, tainted with waste, has backed up over the floor. Still, I am grateful for this hole in the floor, because it means that no matter how much water gushes into this wretched tower, it will eventually all sluggishly drain out again. We will not drown; we will only be miserable. At least we have that much to be grateful for. Misery is to be preferred over death.

I grope to my right and my fingers find the window ledge. It is a small window, grimy and barred, but I sit here often on warm days and read my meagre clutch of letters. It is here that I have stored the small wooden box that contains these precious missives and I am grateful tonight that I did not read them before I fell asleep, otherwise they would have been on the floor beside me. Had they been drenched, I would not have been able to bear their loss. But they are safe. The only lifeline I have to the outside world is safe.

I lean against the damp stone wall and gather my soggy shawl around my shoulders. I am too cold and wet to sleep, so I do what I always do when I am cornered with nowhere else to go. I dream. I rifle through the ageing collection of memories filed neatly in my mind and I pull them out, one after the other. It is these memories that keep me strong. It is by remembering that I am able to steel my resolve even in the worst of times. It is by remembering that I am able to resist.

Le Bouchet, France

January 29, 1719

I am waiting at the window, watching for my brother to come home. My mother is standing by the fireplace stirring a pot of stew.

"Marie," she says quietly. "Come away from the window. Pierre and Papa will be home soon. Come and help me lay the dishes on the table."

I am reluctant to leave my post and I linger a moment before I tear myself away. I push one of the kitchen stools beneath the wooden shelf and then reach up and carefully take down the plates and utensils for dinner. I hop down and begin to lay the table.

"Are we going anywhere tonight, Mama?" I ask, as I concentrate on my task.

My mother is quiet for a moment and then she says, "Why do you ask that?"

I shrug, push back my long brown braid, lay down the last fork and survey my handiwork. "I heard Papa and Pierre whispering to each other this morning," I say.

"Marie!" Mama's tone is gentle but chiding. "You know better than to eavesdrop on conversations that you are not a part of."

I turn to face her then and frown. "I wasn't eavesdropping," I say, tilting my chin just a little. "I was playing with pine cones in the courtyard and Pierre was chopping wood nearby when Papa stopped to talk to him. They could both see me."

Mama smiles and shakes her head. "You are your brother's shadow," she says softly. "Sometimes I think he forgets that you are there at all."

It is true. I adore my brother. I am only eight and Pierre is nineteen and he is my hero. No-one is as tall or as strong as my brother. No-one is as kind or as gentle. But I know he adores me too.

"You still haven't answered my question, Mama," I say. "Are we going somewhere tonight?"

My mother gives the stew a final stir before wrapping her apron around her hand and hefting the pot off the open hearth. She places it on the rough wooden board on the table. "Get the bread," she says to me. I am tempted to stamp my foot and demand an answer to my question, but I know better than to do that. Such behaviour would mean going to bed hungry and the stew smells delicious.

Still frowning, I take the bread and small wooden bowl of butter from the sideboard, my feet tramping a little too loudly across the wooden floor. I put them down on the table a little more forcefully than is necessary and then, feeling my mother's eyes boring into the back of my head, I turn around and shoot her a sheepish look.

"Are you done?" she asks, raising an eyebrow and I know she is not talking about laying out the bread. I open my mouth to answer when I hear laughing voices on the threshold outside. A moment later the door opens and two familiar figures step into the house.

"Pierre!" I squeal, my frustration forgotten. I launch myself at him like a cannon ball and he laughs, gathering me in his arms and swinging me up into the air.

"And how are you, little sparrow?" he asks, as he sets me down on the floor. I launch into an animated story about my day, pausing only to throw myself into my Papa's arms for a big hug. I completely forget about the question I had been asking my mother. As we settle around the table and Papa says grace, I am nearly bursting with joy.

Dinner is, as usual, a noisy affair. Between my wild babbling and the rest of the family trying to get in a few words here and there, we make an animated group. Finally, when we have finished soaking up the last of Mama's stew with hunks of crusty bread, Papa sits back with a satisfied smile on his face and looks around the table at us. "Well, Claudine" he says, smiling affectionately at Mama. "You have outdone yourself once more, my dear. That stew was delicious."

Mama beams at him and rises to begin clearing the dishes. I jump to my feet to help her and, before long, we have cleared the table.

"Where are we meeting?" my mother asks, when we have settled around the table once more.

My eyes go wide and I look from one face to another. *I knew it!* I think triumphantly. I make myself go very still, hoping that they won't stop the conversation because of me.

Pierre glances briefly at me and then looks at my parents. "We are meeting at Michel's," he says.

"Is it safe?' Mama asks.

Pierre purses his lips. "It is as safe as we can make it," he finally says. Then he sighs. "There are spies everywhere, Mama. We do not know who they are but we know they are there. We cannot allow that to stop us from worshipping God."

"I heard rumours of dragoons in the area," Mama says and Papa nods.

"Yes, we have heard reports of patrols."

My eyes go wide. Dragoons are the king's men. I have only seen them a handful of times when I have gone to the market with Mama. I have heard, listening to the hushed whispers of my family talking, that dragoons are sent to take Huguenots away to the galleys.

"We have taken measures to ensure we are safe," Pierre says. "That is why we have chosen the Rouvier farm instead of the woods. They will not be watching for us to gather in someone's home. They are accustomed to us gathering in the woods."

Once, a short while ago, I went for a secret gathering in the woods. Mama woke me up in the middle of the night and quickly helped me slip into my clothes. There was a round full moon hanging low in the sky and Pierre swung me up on his shoulders as we walked through the fields and into the woods. We walked and walked for so long that I began to feel sleepy and I curled myself over the crown of Pierre's head and began to drowse.

When I woke up, we were in a clearing in the woods and I could scarcely believe my eyes. Standing before me was a group of Huguenots. I knew them all because they were friends and neighbours we spent time with. I straightened on Pierre's shoulders and wriggled a little to let him know that I wanted to get down. He obliged and for the rest of the evening I stood beside him, my hand in his, watching in silent awe, as the group sang psalms, read from the Bible and prayed far into the night.

When it was time to go home, Papa gathered me in his arms and I snuggled against his shoulder. As I drifted off to sleep, my mind was filled with the images of that clearing: the lamps hanging from the trees, the soft, low thrum of singing voices and the quiet conviction of the preacher's voice as he read from the Bible.

Coming back to the present from my little reverie, I look carefully around the table at my family. Mama's face looks pale and there are lines creasing her forehead. I can tell that she does not want to go tonight. I look at Papa and I see that his face is as it always is, calm and serene. "We will go," he says softly, and we all know that the matter has been decided for Papa is our leader. We all look to him, even Pierre. Mama's mouth tightens but she says nothing, she only nods.

We go down the narrow steps into the little parlour below the kitchen. Pierre sits crossed-legged on the floor before the hearth and I slip onto his lap. He grins at me and shakes his head. "Always sticking to me like sap," he says with a chuckle.

Papa and Mama sit in the two chairs that face the fire and Papa reads from the worn Bible that he has pulled out of a hidden crevice in the wall. When he has finished reading, we sing psalms and then pray before turning out the lamps and going to bed.

I lie in bed unable to sleep, listening for Mama's footsteps, but they do not come and after a while I find that I cannot keep my eyes open. I am dreaming of dragoons and lanterns when Mama shakes me. I wake up with a start and she gently places her fingers to my lips. "It's time," she says softly. I scramble out of bed and hurry into my clothes. We make our way across the fields to the Rouvier farm in silence. It is a bright night, the moon not quite full but still luminous in the sky.

We have known the Rouvier family almost all our lives. My brother Pierre and Michel Rouvier are close friends and sometimes when I see my brother look at Anne Rouvier, I wonder if he loves her the same way Papa loves Mama, but I'm too shy to ask. When we reach the farm, we huddle against the door and Pierre knocks. I hear a muffled voice from the other side that Pierre answers, then the door swings open.

I am excited to be here. I love these secret night-time gatherings. I love listening to the conversations around me. Most adults don't realise that I am there. I am small and thin for my age. I can fit into a corner and disappear from sight, silently listening. Now as I slip down from Pierre's shoulders I follow Mama, and when she sits beside Madame Rouvier, I quietly take my place on the floor beside them.

"Ah, Claudine, so you have come after all," Madame Rouvier says, when Mama is settled next to her.

"Yes." Mama's voice is always low and gentle. "We are glad you have opened your home to us, Isabeau."

Madame Rouvier shakes her head. "I did not have much choice in the matter," she says. "Michel and your son Pierre had planned everything before I was informed."

Mama is quiet and when I sneak a peek at Madame Rouvier, I see that her face is set in a disapproving frown.

"My Pierre is a good boy, Isabeau," Mama says. "He loves God and has a desire to see the church restored. We have been beaten down to nothing for so long and he is filled with youthful fervour to see the gospel restored in France."

"I do not know if it is fervour or foolishness," Madame Rouvier says with a sniff. "He is putting us all at risk with his ideas. I told Michel to be careful, but he looks up to Pierre so much that he will follow him even to the galleys."

"I pray that never happens," Mama says fervently. I see her watching Pierre, who is at the other end of the room talking to Anne and Michel Rouvier.

"He seems much taken with my Anne," Madame Rouvier observes, following Mama's gaze.

"Anne is a beautiful girl," Mama replies.

"I cannot bear to give her to a man like Pierre," Madame Rouvier says, and I can hear tears in her voice. "Not to a man who is foolish enough to wish to be ordained as a Huguenot pastor. He knows full well that the only end to such a path is death."

"Isabeau. I know that you are...unhappy over our lot in life but that doesn't mean that the work Pierre and others like him are doing is to be despised. There is not a day that goes by that I do not pray for the safety of my son, but I would never ask my boy—as precious as he is to me—to cease his labours. He has been called by God, Isabeau, and even as his mother, it is not my place to intervene."

There is silence then and I quietly watch my brother. My heart swells with pride but also a strange fear. I knew that Pierre wanted to be a pastor. I had heard him speak to Papa about it many times, but I didn't realise that it was dangerous. I wrap my hands around my waist and gently rock back and forth. The thought of losing my brother is more than I can bear, and I want to erase the horrible image from my mind as quickly as I can.

Before long, the meeting starts. Pierre leads us in singing psalms and then he begins to read from the Bible and speak. Everyone is quiet, listening as he speaks about Christ and His great love for us. I am trying to imagine what it must have been like for Jesus to feel the nails piercing His flesh, when we hear a loud crash against the door. I jump and clutch my mother's skirt.

Everyone in the room is frozen in fear. Then we hear a loud voice just beyond the door. "Open in the name of the king!"

The entire room is immediately on its feet and people begin to scramble towards the back of the house. We hear a dull thudding on the front door and the sound of wood splintering. In a moment, Pierre has swung me into his arms and we are running towards the back door. Clinging to his neck, my legs wrapped securely around his waist, I peer over his shoulder. I can see Papa and Mama scrambling behind us, but they are jostled out of the way by others who are desperate to get out.

Suddenly, there is a terrible groaning and the front door gives way. I see the dragoons rush into the room like a flood and I squeeze my eyes shut. Pierre is almost at the door and I feel a rush of cool air on my back. As I open my eyes to see where Papa and Mama are, I see a dragoon grab Mama by her hair and pull her back. She screams, her eyes going wide with terror. Papa turns to go to her, but he is carried forward by the rush of people pushing through the back door. I see Mama struggle against the dragoon and I stretch my hand out towards her screaming, "*Mama! Mama!*"

Pierre stumbles out of the door and we are out in the cold night. Pierre's feet fly beneath him. I hear shouts and screams in the distance, but Pierre keeps running. I close my eyes and cling to him tightly, tears streaming down my face. I am sobbing and whimpering, my face pressed against my brother's neck. All I can see is my mother's face and the face of the dragoon who held her fast, and I know that I will never erase that image from my mind as long as I live.

Suddenly, I hear someone calling Pierre's name. With an extra burst of speed, he ploughs ahead, but the voice behind us is more persistent. And then we both recognise it at the same moment. My head comes up and I reach back. "Papa!" I cry. "Papa!" Pierre slows down a fraction and I hear Papa's ragged breath as he comes abreast of us.

"Give her to me," he gasps, holding his side.

It takes Pierre a moment to realise what he is saying but in a flash, before I have time to react, Pierre has passed me to Papa. I curl around my father and I hear him say, "Go! They will come after you first. You were officiating the meeting. Run hard and hide in the forest." Pierre nods briefly and peels away from us, veering across the darkened fields.

After a while, when it seems as though no-one is following us, Papa lowers me to the ground and kneels before me. I am still crying, almost hysterical, because somehow my young mind knows that I will never see Mama again. Papa tenderly gathers me in his arms and allows me a moment to surrender to my grief. Then he leans away and frames my face with his hands. "Marie," he says gently, "you must be brave."

I draw in a shuddering breath and shake my head. *I can't be brave*, I think. *I can't!* All I want is my Mama. All I want is to be back with my family sitting around the table eating Mama's stew for dinner.

We hurry along in the darkness and find shelter in an abandoned barn. Parts of the roof have burnt away and some of the walls have caved in. The bare bones of its skeleton are exposed to the elements, and we are grateful that it is a clear night, even though it is cold. We lay in the rotting hay that is piled in a corner of the barn. We hear the rustling of mice and the mournful call of an owl fluttering in the rafters. I snuggle next to Papa in the darkness, but neither of us can sleep.

When daylight begins to bleed over the horizon, Papa rises and goes out to check our surroundings. Quietly, we slip over the barren landscape and make our way towards home. From a distance, Papa makes out the hulking forms of two dragoons standing watch beside the door leading into our courtyard. We cannot go home.

For two weeks, we drift around the countryside, sleeping in barns, foraging for food. We do not know where Pierre is. We dare not try to contact any of our Huguenot friends. Finally, the dragoons leave. Papa waits a few more days before we quietly make our way home. I do not know if I will ever feel safe again.

February, 1729

I have not seen my brother in years. Since that awful night so long ago, we have only seen Pierre a handful of times and then only briefly. But we write to each other often. His letters to me keep my hope and my faith alive, and he says my letters do the same for him.

I have worn fear like a shroud around my shoulders for ten long years. I have grown up enmeshed in it, but it has not stripped me of my faith. Perhaps it would have if it had not been for Pierre. My father's faith has wavered and weakened over the years. The trials and hardships we have been forced to face have been too much for him to bear. They have left him bowed down with despair and grey before his time.

We never found out what happened to Mama. That night she melted into the shadows and it is as if she never existed. But we know she lived and was loved. We see her every day when we look into each other's eyes.

Over the fireplace in our kitchen is a short inscription my father carved there years ago. It is now weathered with age but it is still visible, still bearing a silent witness. It reads: "Praise be to God." Four simple words that remind us that even in the midst of suffering and loss, there is still much to be thankful for.

So while I stand at the window waiting for my father to come home, I praise God. "O give thanks unto the Lord for He is good," I murmur, reciting the well-known and well-loved psalm. "For His mercy endures for ever."

And yes, we have seen God's mercy. Pierre is alive and well, even after choosing to defy the king's command and receive ordination as a Huguenot pastor. He now has a bounty on his head that amounts to a small fortune, but he is still alive. And, after loving her for so long, he was finally able to marry Anne Rouvier several years ago. That is something else to be grateful for. Then, as if that were not blessing enough, God has given them children. I adore my nieces and nephews and thank God for them daily, even though I have only seen them on a handful of occasions. Yes, there is much to be grateful for. But more than all these blessings, I am most grateful for my brother's influence in my life. It is Pierre's faith in God that has inspired my own, that has driven me to seek God, to find Him and then to hold on to Him.

I move away from the window and feel a terrible sense of foreboding slither down my spine. *It is not like Papa to be so late*, I think, biting my lower lip. I move down into the small parlour beneath the kitchen. Carefully, my hands move along the rough wall near the hearth till I find the familiar spot I am looking for. I apply pressure in the right places and a panel of the wall gives way, falling easily into my hands. I reach inside the exposed crevice and pull out the heavy family Bible. It is a crime, punishable by death or the galleys, to be in possession of a Bible in the French language. But this Bible is the most precious thing we own. I sit down in Mama's chair and open it. Reverently, I smooth the pages as I turn them, pausing when I come to the passage I am looking for.

My gaze falls over Psalm 61 and I whisper the words to myself in the quiet. "Hear my cry, O God; attend unto my prayer. From the end of the earth will I cry unto thee, when my heart is overwhelmed: lead me to the rock that is higher than I. For thou hast been a shelter for me, and a strong tower from the enemy."

Suddenly, I hear the front door crash open, and I jump so violently that the Bible slips off my lap and thuds to the floor. Then I hear the heavy tread of footsteps in the kitchen above. Panicked, I stare wide-eyed at the landing of the stairway leading upstairs.

"Marie!" I hear Papa call, and I sigh with relief that it is him and that he is home.

"I am here, Papa," I call back, bending to retrieve the Bible and gripping it tightly to my chest.

I hear Papa's footsteps descending the steps rapidly and he strides into the room. One look at his face tells me that my relief must be short lived. "What is it?" I ask. "What has happened?"

He kneels beside my chair and looks into my eyes. "Marie, they are coming for me."

"What?" I ask, confused. "Who? Who is coming, Papa?"

"Monsieur Ladevez, the king's man. He is coming to arrest me."

"What?" I stare at him and shake my head. "No," I say. "No. Why would he arrest you? We haven't been to a gathering in so long. We haven't." Tears are streaming down my face now and I am shaking.

"Marie," Papa grabs my arms. His grip is firm, almost painful, and he forces me to look at him. "I heard from Francois that there were men in the market earlier today asking about me. Specifically, they asked for Durand, the father of the preacher Pierre Durand."

My eyes go wide and I gasp. What will I do if I lose both my father and my brother? I will have no-one left. No-one.

Papa scowls and shakes his head. "I told Pierre not to receive ordination. I told him to stop this foolishness, but he didn't listen and now look at where we are! Have we not suffered enough?"

"Papa." I go to him as he paces restlessly and lay a hand on his arm. "You cannot be angry at Pierre for choosing to share the gospel. You taught him to stand for his faith no matter the cost."

Papa sighs and runs a hand over his face. When he looks at me, I feel as though he has aged a hundred years in a single moment. His face is haggard and weary. "I know," he whispers. "But it is easier to speak of such things while we still have the coins in our hands than after we have paid them." He shakes his head. "It is only a matter of time before someone sends Ladevez and his men here. I waited at the church until they left town and I took the back way home."

"What will we do, Papa?" I ask.

"We must leave," he says softly, determination lighting his eyes. "Go to your room and gather a small bundle of clothing. I will go and see to the mule. We will take the wagon and try to get away."

I look at him doubtfully. *Take the mule and wagon?* I think. I look at my father and he must see the defeat in my face for he takes a step towards me and grips my shoulders. "We cannot simply give up and wait here to be caught," he says. "We must at least *try* to get away."

I nod, gather my courage about me, and run up to my room. I quickly throw some clothes and a small book of psalms into an old sheet and tie off the ends to create a bundle. I then run outside to the stables where I find my father hitching the mule to the wagon in the courtyard.

Suddenly, there is a loud crack and the sound of wood splintering. I scream and my father whirls towards the gate, just as it gives way and crashes open.

"*Run!*" he says to me, pushing me towards the stables. There is a small back door there that leads out into the woods beyond. My eyes widen in terror as I see men emerge from the shadows and march into our courtyard. My father shoves me towards the stables again and turns to face the men.

I run then, fear and guilt roiling through me as my feet pound the cold cobblestones of the courtyard. I hear the men shouting, asking my father to identify himself, asking him to kneel. Tears stream down my face as I fumble with the latch on the gate. I hear footsteps behind me and shouts. I tear the door open and run headlong into the black depths of the night.

I do not know where I am going. My feet fly over the damp earth and the icy wind bites into my cheeks and whips at my hair. I hear shouts behind me, calling for me to stop but I pay them no heed. I keep running. In the distance I can see the dim outline of the woods. I know that if I can reach it I will be safe. *Run, Marie!* I scream to myself. *Run!*

The shouts seem to be getting louder, closer. I press forward, my lungs burning, my legs screaming in pain. I cannot stop. I cannot stop or I know I will die. I hit the treeline of the forest and melt into its shadowy depths, never slowing my pace for even an instant. My heart is thudding so loudly that I fear it will fly straight out of my chest. Suddenly, I feel the ground give way beneath my feet and I land face first in the mud. Panting, I scramble to my feet and look around me. It is pitch dark. There is not even a sliver of moon to light the way and what little light the stars offered out in the open field is now shielded from view by the thick canopy of trees overhead.

I stand still, listening, straining my ears for even the slightest hint of sound that might give away a pursuer—but there is nothing. Only the wind whispering through the trees and the occasional low hoot of an owl. Exhausted, I sink down against the trunk of a nearby tree. My face is hot and my breath comes in ragged gasps, puffing into frosty clouds in the cold night air. My mind is a whirling mess of jumbled, almost incoherent thoughts, but amidst it all a single question begins to fight its way to the surface. *What will they do to Papa?*

Privas, France

April, 1729

I meet Pierre in an abandoned barn on the outskirts of Privas, not far from our home. We meet in the dead of night and only after taking several long circuitous detours to get there. It has taken me two months to get word to my brother about our father's arrest. I have been too afraid to send word, too afraid to do anything but take refuge with a Huguenot family who has kindly offered to shelter me.

When he receives my message, Pierre sends instructions for me to meet him. I approach the abandoned barn quietly, my mind going back to when Papa and I sheltered in a barn just like this on the night that the dragoons came. I enter the dank, rotting structure and make my way to the back corner. The rustle of mice in the hay makes me jump and I fiercely lecture myself to calm down. This is no time to be frightened by obscure noises in the dark. Pierre has a bounty worth thousands of livres on his head. If we are caught, we will both die, but I have to see my brother. He is the only family I have left.

I huddle in a corner and wait. I hear a soft hoot, like that of an owl. My spine stiffens and I listen intently. Two more hoots sound, low and gentle, and I respond. It is a signal that Pierre and I perfected when I was just a little girl. To my right, the shadows move and then my brother appears, his face lit by the waning moon. I jump to my feet and run to him, like I did as a child, and he gathers me in his arms.

"They took him," I sob, clinging tightly to Pierre. "They came and they took him."

"Shhh..." he says softly, gently stroking my hair. After a moment, I draw back and wipe my face with the backs of my hands.

"Did anyone follow you?" Pierre asks, his eyes scanning the barn.

I shake my head. "No," I say. "I am certain."

He nods, then his eyes search my face. "What happened?" he asks. I tell him what little I know, which is that a man called Ladevez came and took Papa.

"They want to force me out of hiding," Pierre says.

"By arresting Papa?" I ask, incredulously.

"Yes." He sighs and motions for me to sit. We sink into the hay, our backs pressed against a crumbling wall. "I received a letter from Ladevez, telling me that if I did not surrender myself, they would arrest Papa."

"But why? They have nothing against him."

"They'll say that he is the father of a Huguenot pastor, but really they are just trying to use my family as a means to get to me. It's me they really want."

I stare at him in shock, as the information slowly takes root in my brain. "Then they will come for me soon," I say softly.

A shadow of emotions dances across Pierre's face: anguish, guilt, anger. He looks away from me and then nods. "Yes, they will. I am glad you contacted me when you did. The safest thing for you to do right now is to come with me. Go into hiding with Anne and the children."

"No," I shake my head. "I cannot. You have enough to worry about trying to protect Anne and the children. If I come to live with you, I will only be adding to your burdens."

"Don't be foolish, Marie," he says gently. "You're my sister. With Papa and Mama both gone, I have a responsibility to take care of you. You are not a burden. You're the only blood family I have left. I can't let anything happen to you."

"And I can't let anything happen to you," I say softly. "If I come, I might slow you down, make things harder. I can't do that, Pierre. If something were to happen to you, where would I be? We only have each other now."

"So then what are you suggesting? Surely you don't expect me to leave you with Francois and Marienne? They have been kind enough to welcome you into their home these last two months, but that arrangement cannot go on forever."

"No," I say slowly. "It cannot. Which is why I have a plan."

"A plan?" Pierre raises an eyebrow at me and even in the dim light filtering through the gaping wall, I can see the caution in his eyes. "What kind of plan?"

"Matthew Seres." I say the name, watching for his reaction.

"Matthew Seres?" Pierre's voice is full of disbelief. "I thought I had convinced Papa to abandon that idea."

I shake my head. "No, he was actively pursuing it when he was taken."

Pierre jumps to his feet and begins to pace in front of me. He pushes a hand through his hair and blows out his breath, the air white in front of his face. "He is almost twenty years older than you, Marie. I told Papa…I told him that he could not sell you to that man."

"No-one is selling me," I say, standing to my feet and facing him. "Matthew is a good man. A man of our faith. He approached Papa about marrying me months ago and it seemed to be a good fit."

"A good fit for whom?" Pierre asks. "Papa? So he could have the assurance that his daughter would be taken care of should something happen to him?"

"Can you blame him?" I lay a gentle hand on his arm. "Pierre, I am not in a position to choose, to wait for something like you and Anne have. Perhaps in another world, another lifetime, I too could have found the kind of love that you have found with Anne, but the way things are…" I pause and take in a steadying breath. "Matthew is a kind man. He cares for me and he will protect me and provide for me. That is all that I can hope for."

"You deserve more, little sparrow," he says softly.

"But this is what God has given me and I must believe that it is the best that I can have," I say.

He smiles at me—a small, sad smile—and I return it.

Le Bouchet, France
Spring, 1730

I am at home, the home I share with my new husband Matthew, when the guards come. We are having dinner quietly, when they break open the door and train their pistols on us and ask us to stand. I have known that this day would come for a long time. I have seen it approach in the distance, like a terrible black cloud, but when it finally arrives, I still find that I am not ready for it.

"Durand?" one of the men asks.

Matthew is quick to answer. "No," he says, shaking his head. "We are not Durand. We are Seres. I am Matthew Seres and this is my wife, Madame Seres."

They look confused for a moment, until I quietly shake my head. "I am Durand," I say, contradicting my husband. I cannot renounce my brother. I cannot hide behind my new husband's name and pretend that I am not the sister of one of the most faithful and godly men that France has ever seen. "I am Marie Durand."

"Is Pierre Durand your brother?" he asks me, looking at Matthew with a satisfied smirk.

"Yes," I say. "Pierre Durand is my brother."

"Marie!" Matthew's voice is sharp. I turn towards him and shake my head. "They may take me to the galleys or burn me at the stake, Matthew," I say steadily, "but there are two things I will never deny. I will never deny my faith and I will never deny my brother."

But they do more than just arrest me. They arrest Matthew as well. They take him to the tower where Papa is imprisoned. They will not spare him, because he is the brother-in-law of a known outlaw. I am appalled and wracked with guilt. I might not be in love with Matthew but he is a good man. He offered me a home and shelter when I had nowhere else to go and I feel as though my impulsive decision to acknowledge my brother has hurt an innocent man.

They take me to Aigues-Mortes, to the Tower of Constance. When I see the circular stone structure rising before me, I feel as though I might faint. I have heard stories of this place. *Oh Lord!* I think, a sob rising in my throat. *Oh Lord, give me strength, for I do not have the strength to bear this.*

We walk up the stone steps and pause before the locked door. Above it are engraved the words: "All hope abandon, ye who enter here." As I read it, a steely resolve rises up in my heart in answer to my prayer. *No!* I think. *You may imprison my body, but you can never have my heart. I will not yield my hope. I will resist.*

When they enter my name on the roll, they do not enter Marie Seres. I ask that they enter Marie Durand. I will bear that name till the day I die. If I am remembered, then I want those who read the roll to know who I am and what I stood for. I am Marie Durand. I will resist.

Aigues-Mortes, France
Spring, 1745

It is still raining and I am freezing. The stream of water pouring through the hole in the roof has not yet eased enough for the water around my ankles to dissipate. For now, there is nowhere dry in this place. We just have to wait for the water to subside. I pull my wet shawl closer around me and bounce a little, trying to warm up. Eventually the rain ceases and dawn begins to colour the small circle of sky above us and I welcome the light.

I reach up and finger the box that is perched on the ledge beside me. It is still too dark to read, but soon it will be light enough and I will take out each letter and read them over again. They are all that I have left of my brother. He was arrested and hanged thirteen years ago now, two years after my imprisonment. My sister-in-law Anne wrote that he went without fear and sang on his way to the gallows. "God gave him to me," she wrote, the ink blotted where her tears had fallen on the page, "and He has taken him away. His will be done."

I thought I had no tears left, but when I received Anne's letter, I wept as though I had an endless reservoir. My beloved brother was gone and I would never see his face again. But even in the midst of my mourning, my heart was filled with pride. Pierre Durand was a man who refused to surrender his faith, even at the cost of his life. And so I will not surrender mine, even though it has cost me my freedom.

During the fifteen years I have spent imprisoned in this wretched tower, I have not been idle. There is much to be done here. The weak and elderly need to be cared for. So I have written letters, so many letters. We place them in a small box and lower it through the bars of the window with a ribbon to friends who stand below, ready to take them and dispatch them. I have written to every Huguenot pastor I know, pleading for supplies: blankets, clothing, anything they can spare. The supplies have been smuggled back to us when the guards were not watching.

Small copies of the gospels and psalms have also been smuggled in and, each morning, before the guards come to check on us, we spend time in prayer and song. In every way I know, I resist. By writing letters, by reading Scripture, by nurturing the faith of my fellow prisoners, I resist the tyranny that has stripped us of our freedom and, in so doing, I preserve my own faith.

A rustle beside me brings me out of my reflection. I turn my head and smile at the woman who has crept up to me. She is pale and gaunt, her cheeks sunken and her hair a thin smattering of grey strands pulled tightly away from her face.

"Mama Isabeau," I say, smiling and reaching my hand out to her. Pierre's mother-in-law and I were brought to the tower around the same time. She was arrested for the same reason I was, for being related to the infamous Pierre Durand.

"How are you?" I ask gently, massaging her freezing hand as it grasps mine. She coughs, a dry rattle that sounds deep in her chest.

"That water did me no good," she says, pulling her shawl tightly around her shoulders.

"We will see if we can get some warm blankets from the guards when they come to bring us food," I tell her.

"The king's intendant is visiting us today," she reminds me, and I nod. He is coming to offer freedom in exchange for a signed recantation or attendance at mass. She is silent for a moment. "Have you thought about what you will do?" she asks.

"I won't recant," I say.

She shakes her head at me. "We will die in this tower, Marie, and for what? For our ideals? What did our ideals do for us last night while we were drowning in rainwater and sludge?" She looks away.

"So you will recant then?" I ask, more curious to hear her response than to respond to her frustrations.

"I don't know," she says, her eyes still averted. "Are you sure that you will not recant?" she asks again. She is like a child who wants to play but is too afraid to go out alone.

"I already said I wouldn't," I say with a small smile.

"You are like your brother," she says with a condescending sniff. "Always more worried about doing what is right than doing what is necessary."

"Why must they be different? Isn't it necessary to do what is right?"

"Because doing what is right doesn't always turn out well," she says. "Look at us." She waves a bony arm around the tower, taking in the groups of women, whose dim outlines we can now make out in the early morning light. Like us, they are drenched and shivering, huddled in groups or by themselves.

"We are like vermin or even worse. And for what? Because we read the Bible in French and refuse to attend a mass. Why should these be punishable crimes?"

"Because the king says they are," I reply.

She sighs. "The king holds our fate in his hands. If we disagree with him, then this is what he does to us."

"He can imprison us, Mama Isabeau, but he can't touch our hearts or our minds." I clench my fists. "He can ask us to abandon our hope when we enter this place, but he can't reach into our hearts and wrench it out. Not unless we let him and I, for one, am not willing to let him."

"So you will die here?" she asks.

"If I have to," I say. "I have been here for fifteen years and if God sees fit to leave me here another fifteen, then I will bear it. But I can't exchange the freedom of my conscience for freedom from these walls." I turn to look at her then. "Why have you not recanted before?" I ask her. "You have been in this tower almost as long as I have. You have had ample opportunity to leave. So why are you still here, asking me if I will recant when you have never done so?" There is no condemnation in my voice. I am just curious.

She sighs. "Because when they first brought me here I was like you. I refused to let them take away my faith. And then I refused to

147

let them take away my freedom. And then I refused to let them break my spirit. But now, when I can hear the rattle of death in my lungs, I wonder, is this where I want to die? After all these years of resisting what have I to look forward to?"

I squeeze her hand tight. "A better country," I say, thinking of the book of Hebrews. "Your resistance has given you hope for a better country and a better city whose builder and maker is God. That is what you have to look forward to, Mama Isabeau—a better land."

She is quiet for a long time and then slips away from me without a word. I watch her go. She moves to a part of the room that she has claimed as her own and lays down on the sodden blanket there, her body shaking as she coughs.

I am suddenly gripped by a ferocious determination. As I watch her, as I watch the faces of the other women around me, I think, *They cannot have us. They can wear us down and treat us like animals, but they cannot tear away our hope.*

I think of my favourite psalm once more and recite the words in my heart: "Hear my cry, O God; attend unto my prayer. From the end of the earth will I cry unto thee, when my heart is overwhelmed: lead me to the rock that is higher than I. For thou hast been a shelter for me, and a strong tower from the enemy." As long as I have Christ, I have everything I will ever need. He is the rock that is higher than the roiling emotions that churn within me and the wretched conditions that plague us in this tower.

I stand up and go to my box. Reaching inside, I pull out a sharp nib that I use for my writing. Turning around, I stride to the refuse hole in the centre of the room and lower myself to the floor beside it. Then I begin to painstakingly scratch out a single word in the rim, gritting my teeth with determination. Slowly, the word begins to form, scraped into the stone by sheer force of will. It is a single word that helps me to remember what I must do when I face the intendant later today and what I must do in order to preserve those things that are most dear to my heart. One word: *Resist.*

Later that day, Monsieur Lenain, the king's intendant, comes to the tower. He sees us one by one and presents us with a recantation to sign. There are thirty-one of us imprisoned there for our faith and when he leaves, only eight of us remain.

That evening, as the sun wanes, I crawl over to the refuse hole and finger the word I have scratched into the rim.

"What is it, child?" Mama Isabeau asks, crouching beside me.

"A reminder," I say, looking at her and smiling. I take her hand and squeeze it. "A reminder of what we did today and what we must continue to do every day for Christ."

Slowly, we make our way back to the remaining six women and huddle together in preparation for another night together in the tower. Closing my eyes, I quietly repeat the words I chanted to myself when they first brought me here: *Je suis Marie Durand. Je vais resister.*

I am Marie Durand. I will resist.

Marie Durand (1711–1776) was imprisoned in the Tower of Constance in 1730, in response to the illegal ordination and ministry of her elder brother, Pierre. Despite the terrible conditions she experienced in the tower, Marie did not recant her faith, even though she had many opportunities to do so. Instead, she became a champion for the women who were imprisoned with her, writing to friends to ask for supplies for their comfort and even for copies of the Scriptures. She often led the women in worship and prayer, encouraging them to remain steadfast in their faith. She was released on April 14, 1768, after thirty-eight years in the tower. Her inscription, Resister (Resist), can still be seen etched in the stone of the tower today.

7

Katherine Parr
THE SURVIVOR

London, England

April, 1543

I have caught the attention of the wife killer and now I am trapped like a mouse. When he asks me to marry him, I cannot speak. I stand there staring at him until I feel my sister's elbow digging sharply into my side. I finally dip into a low curtsey. "You...you flatter me, Your Majesty," I murmur, my head bowed towards the ground.

He grunts and then laughs. "I expect you are beside yourself with joy, eh?" he says, and all his courtiers titter alongside him. I feel my cheeks grow hot and I keep my head low, praying that he will indeed think that I am beside myself with joy and not realise that I am actually beside myself with dread.

"Rise, rise, Lady Latimer," he says to me. I slowly rise, my hands clasped nervously in front of me. "You need not answer my suit today." He waves a large meaty hand in front of him airily, and I suppress the urge to shudder.

He is a large man, tall and broad, and I cannot help but think of his big hand squeezing my slender neck. To say that I am afraid of him would be an understatement. He is imposing in every way, not only in size but also in presence. There is something about him that is menacing. His face is large and round, his double chin puffed out a little, making his lips look thin and small. His eyes are beady, darting around beneath his jewelled cap, taking my measure as though I were a piece of meat at the butchers.

Of all the women he could have cast his eyes on, it is I who now face the peril of becoming his sixth wife. For I know as surely as the sun rises in the east, that I cannot refuse him. No-one refuses this king. I do not think anyone has refused him anything since he was a child. When Henry wants something, he gets it, even if he has to wade through blood to secure it.

I manage to mumble some sort of promise about giving him my answer before long, then I leave the room as quickly as decorum will permit. My sister Anne takes my hand and leads me through the maze of galleries and hallways at Hampton Court Palace, until we are in her rooms. Then she closes the door behind us and we face each other.

"You do not have to look so pale, Kate," she tells me wryly. "It is not as though he is sending you to the Tower."

"Maybe not now," I fire back. "But that is what happened to his last wife."

She sighs and rolls her eyes, moving towards the window embrasure and beckoning me to join her. "Katherine Howard was a little fool," she says dismissively, "and you are nothing like her."

"Well, we have the same name," I observe.

Anne laughs. "Do you know that when you marry him you will be the third Katherine he has taken to wife? Do you suppose he has some sort of affinity for that name?" I notice that she says *when* I marry him and not *if*.

"Do you suppose I could say no, Nan?" I ask, and she stares at me as though I have taken leave of my senses.

"Why would you want to do that?" she asks.

"Given what has happened to four of his previous five wives I think that I have cause for concern," I say peevishly.

"It is not as though he killed them all," she says.

"No," I concede. "But he harassed poor Queen Katherine right into her grave. He could not lay an axe to her neck for fear of what her nephew the emperor might do to England, but had she been an Englishwoman, he would have killed her and been done with it. Instead he tore her away from her only child, flaunted his mistress before her eyes, demanded a divorce and banished her to die in the damp confines of Kimbolton Castle." I am breathless as I recount the sad tale of Queen Katherine of Aragon.

"Our lady mother, bless her, adored that woman," Anne says. Queen Katherine was my godmother and I am named for her. Our mother was one of her ladies-in-waiting and a much beloved one.

"And what about the next wife?" I continue after a brief reprieve. "He fought and fought for her, turned England and all Christendom upside down to have her, and then what? No sooner had he married her than he had her beheaded on trumped up charges of adultery."

"She couldn't give him a son," Anne says, as though this explains everything.

"And just because Queen Anne could not give him a son did that give him the right to kill her?" I ask. Anne shoots me a warning glare and I know that I am treading on thin ice. It is forbidden to speak ill of the king and here I am blabbering like a seditious fool, but I cannot help it. If I do not give voice to my fears, they will overwhelm me and I cannot afford to be overwhelmed now.

"You have nothing to worry about, Katie," Anne says soothingly. "He has no need of an heir now. Queen Jane gave him one and there is Lady Mary and Lady Elizabeth besides. I do not think he will expect much from you, just companionship perhaps."

I shake my head. King Henry VIII has beheaded two wives, another two he has all but killed from neglect and one he has put aside and now calls his beloved sister. Had she not agreed to go quietly, I am sure he would have found a reason to kill her as well. And now he wants to make me his sixth queen. I cannot help but wonder what my end will be. Will I survive him or, as seems to be the case with this king, will he survive me?

Summer, 1543

I have put him off for two months and thankfully he is not pressuring me. Anne says it is because he knows I will not refuse him. I do not know if I should be relieved or alarmed that he is so sure of my consent. I am beginning to think that I might drag my feet forever when my siblings decide to intervene. I am at the Charterhouse, my home in London, when they come to me, looking equally determined.

"Now, Kate," my brother William begins, "surely you do not mean to refuse him? He is King of England. No woman in her right mind would think to refuse such an offer."

"I am tired of being married," I hedge, and Anne rolls her eyes at me. "It is true!" I say. "I have been twice married and though neither has been an unpleasant experience, I am content as I am. My husband, Lord Latimer, left me enough means to live comfortably. You know that. I have a good jointure and he bequeathed other estates besides."

"And you think that being the comfortably-provided-for widow of John Neville, Lord Latimer, is a more desirable prospect than being the Queen of England?" William looks at me in disbelief.

I sigh. I know what is expected of me. If I were to become Queen of England, William would be given a peerage and Anne's husband would be given a title. Even though I do not want the position myself, I know that I must take it for the sake of my family.

"Is there someone else?" William asks, his eyes narrowing suspiciously as the silence lengthens.

"No," I say quickly, perhaps too quickly. There is someone else but it does not matter. No other suitor would ever stand in the way of King Henry VIII.

"You know what you must do," William says.

I nod, for there is nothing else I can do. "I cannot do it alone," I say, looking at Anne, my eyes beseeching.

"Of course not," she says, coming to me, her hands outstretched. I take them and give them a squeeze. We have always been close—the three Parr siblings. "I have been lady-in-waiting to every one of King Henry's queens," Anne says softly. "It will be a privilege to serve my own sister in that capacity."

I smile at her and nod. I know what I must do. But why do I feel as though I am being led to the gallows to do it?

July 12, 1543

We are married in the small private chapel just above the Chapel Royal at Hampton Court on a hot summer day. It feels even hotter because I am draped in heavy gold cloth, brocade and satin. My train is more than two yards long and it all weighs on me. The king stands before me and clasps my tiny hand in his large palm. He towers over me like a gigantic oak—thick and broad and tall—and for a single irrational moment I am tempted to run.

We are being married by special licence, having dispensed with the usual ceremony of the banns—three consecutive public announcements of our intent to marry. The Archbishop of Canterbury, Dr Thomas Cranmer, has issued us with the licence but we are to be married by the Bishop of Winchester, Stephen Gardiner. It is a curious mixture of clergy. Dr Cranmer is a reformist and a closeted follower of Dr Martin Luther, whom my new groom hates with a passion. On the other hand, the Bishop of Winchester is an adherent of the old religion and as wily and as conniving as any bishop in Christendom. I realise there is much to learn if I am to survive at court.

The mixture of attendees testifies of the king's continued religious confusion. Henry is like a child who cannot decide what he wants, so instead he has decided he would like a little bit of everything. He threw out the pope so he could divorce Queen Katherine and declared himself the head of the Church of England, as it has become known, but this did not mean he adopted the reformed faith. He quite likes certain parts of it, like giving the people the Bible in the English language. But there are parts of the new movement of reform that he seems to despise, like Martin Luther's teachings about justification by faith. Henry finds comfort in believing that his own works will get him into heaven. He has great faith in himself.

I am not entirely sure what I believe and, in that sense, I am much like my groom. My late husband, Lord Latimer, was strongly aligned to the old religion but the family of my first husband, Edward Borough, had reformist leanings. They had a copy of the Bible in their home. My own brother is reformist minded. As yet, I am undecided, I suppose. I read the Bible on occasion but not fervently. I attend mass daily, but so do most people in England, including the king.

The bishop begins in a droning voice and I feel the king's grip on my hand tighten. I sneak a peek at him from beneath my lashes and find that he is watching Stephen Gardiner with rapt attention. I am relieved. I do not think I can bear any more of his scrutiny, for he has been watching me as a wolf watches a lamb it is stalking for lunch. Bishop Gardiner is now asking the king to repeat his vows.

"I, Henry, take thee, Katherine," his voice booms and I try not to flinch or shiver, "to be my wedded wife, to have and to hold from this day forward for better or worse..." They are words I have heard before and I am barely paying attention, waiting for the last part, the part that I fear most: "till death us do part and thereto I plight thee my troth."

I swallow hard and begin to repeat my vows back to him, nearly choking on the words "till death us do part." I wonder if the irony is lost on him. He has repeated these vows six times now and each time he has walked away unscathed, while his brides have plighted their troth to him at the peril of their own lives.

When we are done and the wedding rings have been exchanged, I turn to my sister and hug her tightly. "All will be well," she murmurs to me. "You will see." My brother is not with us today and I miss him.

I receive well wishes from the Earl and Countess of Hertford and then the Duke and Duchess of Suffolk. I smile at the countess and the duchess for I know that they will soon join my staff as ladies-in-waiting. Both Anne Seymour and Katherine Brandon smile back warmly but there is a glimmer of acid behind Anne Seymour's eyes that makes me recoil inwardly. I think she is one I will have to watch. But the young Duchess of Suffolk, Katherine Brandon, is genuinely pleased and I take an immediate liking to her.

There is no fanfare after our wedding. No wine flowing in fountains or loud processions through the streets of London. I am not even crowned. Instead, I am proclaimed Queen of England later that day and it is enough for me. There has been enough trouble over the queens of England this past decade to last us all a lifetime and more. We do not need further ado over the newest head to wear the crown.

Royal progress

Summer to Autumn, 1543

As it happens, my new husband and I have an extended honeymoon. The plague is sweeping through London leaving cartloads of dead in its wake. The king is terrified of disease of any kind and immediately decides to leave on progress to get as far away as possible from the fetid London air and dying Londoners in general. He decrees that no Londoner is to come within seven miles of the royal person, so the entire court is forced to pack up and leave with him or risk being left behind. In Henry's England, there is nothing worse for a courtier than to be left behind.

The plague is particularly virulent this year and we are forced to go on progress for a good six months, but I do not mind this. It gives me an opportunity to understand court life and, more importantly, to understand my new husband. I find that he is not as fearful as I had first thought and though I do not fall in love with him, I find that my affection for him grows.

The happiest part of being Queen of England is my new role as step-mother to Henry's children. Lady Mary and Lady Elizabeth were at our wedding and at court just prior to it, so I have had the opportunity to get to know them. My heart goes out to both of them.

Mary is twenty-seven, only three years younger than I am, so I must treat her more as a friend than a daughter. But she is open to my friendship. In fact, she seems to welcome it. I suppose she reserved all her animosity for Queen Anne, who took her mother's place as Queen of England. Henry has been nothing short of tyrannical in his treatment of Lady Mary. First, he tore her away from her mother, then he stripped away her closest companions and the most trusted members of her household, then he hounded her to deny her mother and her own birthright as Princess of England. She is known as the Lady Mary because her father has declared her illegitimate, though how such a thing is possible none of us knows, for he was married to her mother when she was born. But then it seems that this king makes up facts to suit his own fancy and no-one can contradict him. If he were to tell us the sky is green, we could not deny it, for otherwise he might send us to the Tower to have our heads lopped off for treason.

Then there is young Lady Elizabeth. She was just two and a half when her mother was beheaded and she was declared illegitimate. She is a pale little thing of nine years, serious and staid. She has only known the care of one governess after another. At least Lady Mary knew a mother's love, but not little Elizabeth. I am instantly drawn to her and take her under my wing. I determine that I shall be a mother to her. I have had practise. My second husband, Lord Latimer, had two children when I married him. In fact, his daughter Margaret is even now with me at court and I am her mother in every way that matters.

Finally, there is the young Prince Edward, the long-sought-for boy. There are times when it seems as though the king has offered up his wives before some pagan god like Chemosh or Baal in order to sire this son. Perhaps I exaggerate, but it has cost the lives of three wives to produce this single pale-faced heir. Edward is five when I first meet him at Ashridge, where he and Lady Elizabeth share a household. Edward's sisters dote on him. In fact, all three Tudor children seem to adore one another. Mary especially dotes on her two younger siblings, as though they are her own children.

Edward is kept as far away from London as possible and is treated as though he were the most fragile flower in Christendom. No-one is to come near the little prince unless they have received special permission to attend him and his food is meticulously tasted before it is presented to him. His laundry is subjected to the most rigorous standards of hygiene before his clothes are allowed anywhere near him. Indeed, it is as though he is made of glass and even the slightest breath might crack and shatter him irretrievably.

I suppose this is to be expected. But the weight of being the only living Tudor heir presses on the shoulders of this five-year-old boy, making him seem ten times his age. Although I do not have children of my own, every maternal instinct in my heart is aroused when I see little Edward. He greets me and his father so formally and in such perfect Latin. When I see the cold, formal way in which Henry interacts with him, I long to run to him and fold him in my arms. He is still a little boy but he is treated as though he is a man.

I ask him if I may exchange letters with him. "Indeed, lady mother," he says to me, his little face solemn. "I would be honoured to correspond with your grace." I offer him a small smile and glance at his father to see if he will object, but he does not say anything and I am satisfied. We agree to write to each other in Latin and it is only later that I realise that my Latin is actually quite appalling. I will need to find myself a tutor if I am to properly correspond with my little prince.

London, England
December, 1543

We are back at Hampton Court for Christmas and there is much that needs attending to. I have settled on who will attend me in my rooms and I find that court life is a delicate balance.

"You can't only have people you are comfortable with," Anne tells me with a grin. "You need to have ladies in your household whose husbands serve the king. That is to your advantage."

"For gossip to travel?" I ask dryly.

"Yes," she concedes. "But gossip travels both ways you know, and it is always good to have a finger on this particular king's pulse. One never knows when one will be called upon to spring into action."

I study my sister for a moment. "Was that what it was like with the other queens?" I ask.

Anne shrugs. "Queen Katherine never saw it coming. I mean she knew the king had his eye on Anne Boleyn, but she never thought he would turn on her the way he did. He rode away from her one day without saying goodbye and that was that."

I find that I am mildly obsessed with the wives that have gone before me, perhaps because I do not want to repeat their mistakes. "And Queen Anne?" I ask my sister.

She sighs. "One thing you must learn about this king, Kate," she says, "is that he enjoys throwing everyone off kilter. None of his wives really knew what he was thinking and none of them ever suspected what would befall them. Henry is good at sweet-talking anyone and everyone. He is good at being two-faced." She lowers her voice. "And you would do well to remember that."

This is my first Christmas as queen and I am glad to have all three of the royal children with us at court. It is the first Christmas in a long time that Henry's children have all been with him and we make a happy family. The children seem to genuinely enjoy being with their father, and I try to make the festive season as happy and as meaningful for them as possible. More and more, I find that I am becoming comfortable around the king, and more and more, I find myself falling deeply in love with his three children.

Summer, 1544

I have discovered a new passion. Here at court, as Queen of England, I feel as though I have all the scholarship of the world at my fingertips and it leads me to rediscover the Bible. It is not as though I have never had access to it—I have—but here in this new world I find myself in, I have the freedom and the time to explore it more deeply. I begin to relish each moment I spend combing its pages.

But even more of a delight is the time that I spend conversing about it. My rooms are filled with ladies who are reform minded: the Countess of Hertford, Anne Seymour; the Duchess of Suffolk, Katherine Brandon; my own sister. Soon we are diligently studying the Scriptures and talking about what we have learned together. These are precious times, golden hours that we spend not in secret, not having to hide what we are doing, but openly, inside my own rooms.

Often when my husband visits me, I find that I cannot keep myself from sharing what we are learning. The king is a jovial man but he is also incredibly intelligent, and I find myself drawn into deep theological discussions with him. I enjoy them and I am led to believe that he does too.

My ladies and I undertake a project that brings me further joy. I begin to translate a small book called *Psalms and Prayers* from the Latin into English. Dr Cranmer passes it to me, discreetly of course. We are very careful about who knows of our connection to each other. He is staunchly reform minded and I am fast becoming the same, but the court of King Henry VIII is rife with political machination and we cannot be seen to be allied too closely. There are factions at court divided along religious lines and those of the old religion are deeply interested in winning and keeping the favour of the king and perhaps returning England to the bosom of the pope. Henry will have none of this idea.

There are times when I am tempted to believe it is because he truly cares about reform, times when our discussions on theology lead me to think that he is as deeply affected by these things as I am. Then there are other times when I wonder if he just enjoys being pope over the English church more than anything else, for that is what he has made the Church of England. It is a church of the old religion with free access to the Bible and a new pope, King Henry himself.

He burns Catholics as freely as he burns Lutherans, for no-one is ever quite certain where he has drawn the lines of religious belief and then they overstep them and pay the price. Catholics burn for wanting a return to Rome and Lutherans burn for denouncing the mass. No-one is really safe to think for themselves, so we must all try to find out what the king is thinking and think like him. But in the privacy of my rooms, when we are discussing theology, I forget all this and freely speak my mind. He does not seem to be troubled by it and I think, *Surely he will not behead me for speaking my mind? Surely not. I am, after all, Queen of England.*

My sister tells me that I am a fool to think this way, but I am not convinced enough by her arguments to listen. It is not that I am in love with Henry. I do not think that I could love a man who has beheaded two of his wives. But I am not as afraid of him as I once was and he seems to be growing on me. There are times when I see the golden prince again, for that is what Henry once was. When his miserly father Henry VII died and Henry VIII took the throne at just eighteen, he was hailed as the golden prince: the liberal one, the compassionate one and the handsome one. He was England's pride and joy until suddenly he became the tyrant who would wade through blood for a son and heir.

So I allow myself to let down my guard when I am with him and share all that I am learning, even though there are reformists who are burned at Smithfield with increasing frequency. And then, as though to confirm the king's trust in me, he names me regent when he decides to invade France. Of course, everyone is terrified about his mad bid to try to reclaim English land in France. It seems impossibly foolish. He is a giant of a man with weak legs. He is constantly in pain and can barely walk alone. If he were to kneel, he would need at least three men to help him stand again, if not more. So how will he fare in France, we think? But he does not like to accept that he is ageing and he wants one final chance at glory. A final hurrah where he is able to thumb his nose at Francis I of France, his long-time rival. Another Field of the Cloth of Gold or—heaven forbid that he should be so foolish, but we think that he might be—another Agincourt, where he can display his splendour and the military superiority of England.

The last time he went to war and named his queen regent in his absence was when Mary's mother, Queen Katherine, was alive and pregnant with their child. Katherine ruled England and fended off an invasion by the Scots. James IV of Scotland was killed and she sent his bloodied jacket to her husband in France as a token of the victory. She was in every way her mother's daughter, ruling with the iron savagery of Isabella of Castile.

But I am not *that* Queen Katherine. I am a gentlewoman from the north of England, whose mother was a lady-in-waiting to a queen, but I am determined to be a good regent nonetheless. Of course, my husband does not leave me to rule alone in his absence. He gives me a council to support me. We are all aware of the constant threat to our northern border from Scotland and there are times when I wonder what I would do if the Scots were to invade again, as they did all those years ago.

I find that this is a time when I turn to Scripture more frequently. I spend time on my knees. I feel that if ever I needed the presence and strength of God to guide me and give me wisdom, it is now. My time as regent strengthens my faith, strengthens my personal connection with God. This is what I love most about being a reformist, it puts me in direct communion with God. I do not need a priest or a host. I can come before my God and lay my petitions at his feet. I can know for certain that he hears my prayers without any human intercessor. It is like walking into a strange new world full of exciting possibilities, a world I never want to leave.

I bring Elizabeth and Edward to Hampton Court so that we are all together while the king is away. It is a special time for all of us. Mary is with me in my rooms and we make a happy family. Henry has recently restored both Mary and Elizabeth to the line of succession after Edward and I know, given the uncertain times in which we live, that it is possible that all three of them may one day rule England. Mary is a Romanist, but I am determined that Elizabeth and Edward are raised as reformists. Edward is first in line to the throne after his father and I want him to be a true reformist king. While my duties as regent occupy much of my time, I make it a point to ensure that the young prince and princess receive an education at the hands of some of the most learned reformist thinkers in England.

At the same time, my ladies and I continue our afternoon discussions in my rooms and work on our translation. I love this work. It is a joy for me to write, to take pains to ensure that the proper meaning of the words are conveyed, that nothing is lost in translation. It is tedious work but exhilarating and rewarding at the same time. During our discussions, my ladies suggest that we should invite reformist speakers to preach to us on occasion and I am thrilled with the idea. Slowly, we begin to open my rooms to reformist preachers who come in the afternoon hours and speak to us from the Scriptures, expounding truths and challenging our thinking in ways that we would not have imagined.

I find that my time as regent has not only strengthened me as a woman and a queen, but it has also strengthened my faith. For the first time since my marriage to the king, I feel as though I am truly Queen of England. I have a sense of assurance and boldness that I have not felt before. I have guarded my husband's lands and his children in his absence, as a good wife ought, and I am sure to irrevocably secure his favour.

Spring, 1545

I am about to go to the king's rooms at Whitehall Palace to see him before dinner when my lady the Duchess of Suffolk curtseys before me.

"Your Highness," she says, and I pause at the door of my presence chamber and motion for her to rise.

"What is it, Lady Suffolk?" I ask her.

"A word in your ear, if I may?" I nod and motion to a window embrasure near us.

When we are seated inside, she leans close to me and whispers, "I have found someone you might be interested in." I raise an eyebrow and smile benignly. Katherine Brandon has been part of my household since I became queen. Her husband, the doddering old Charles Brandon, is Henry's greatest friend. He is the only man at court who dares to speak his mind, and he addresses the king as "Harry" more often than not. Henry loves him and has only gone so far as to banish him from court when he has overstepped his bounds.

Katherine is nearly twenty-five years younger than him, and she is intelligent, witty and outspoken. Over the years, we have become fast friends and somewhat united in our dislike of Stephen Gardiner, the Bishop of Winchester. Now, in her quiet, earnest voice she tells me of Anne Askew, a young woman from Lincolnshire who has lately come to London. Her sister is married to a lawyer in Katherine Brandon's household and so Katherine has had an opportunity to meet with her.

"She is a reformist," Katherine says to me, "and I thought that perhaps you might be interested in listening to her one afternoon."

I consider this for a moment. "Are there any risks?" I ask finally, and Katherine nods slowly. "She is outspoken in her denunciation of the mass, but your Highness, she is one of the best expositors of the Bible I have heard. She is as well read and witty as any man, and she speaks the truth with such power that I believe it would be worth the risk to have her, perhaps for a single afternoon or two. We could take certain precautions to make sure that her visit is not too conspicuous."

The king is only too happy to burn anyone who denounces the mass, but there are so many who are reformist minded who do. In Henry's mind, as in the mind of every other Catholic in Christendom, the mass is the sacrament of sacraments. To every adherent of the old religion, the moment when the priest recites his Latin incantation over the bread, it becomes the very body of Christ. Of course, every reformist denies this. To them the mass is nothing more than a mummery and to believe that the host transforms into the body of Christ is the height of idolatry. Henry has been all too happy to rid England of the pope, but he cannot countenance ridding England of the mass.

I am tempted to take the safe path and tell my lady of Suffolk that we dare not risk it, but I am too curious to hear Anne Askew speak and so in the end I agree. We will see her but discreetly. She is to come quietly by the river and then make her way to my rooms through a concealed entrance. She is to speak to us in broad daylight in the very midst of my presence chamber so no-one can accuse us of any clandestine meetings, but we will make sure that few people know that she is here.

When Anne Askew comes, she sets us all ablaze. As Katherine Brandon has said, she is well read and witty and her knowledge of the Bible is astounding. She is able to answer our questions without batting an eye and to expound Scripture in the most thorough manner imaginable. She quotes passages of the Bible from memory and we are enthralled by it all. Even Princess Mary, sitting quietly at the back of the room, listens with rapt attention. We are careful to stay away from topics that the king has expressly forbidden, but there is so much to talk about on a range of other topics that we hardly notice the restriction.

I invite Anne to speak to us on several occasions until we hear that she has been arrested and questioned by the Bishop of London. It is then that my sister Anne comes to me concerned.

"You cannot be seen fraternising with her, Katie," she tells me once we are in my privy chamber and the doors are locked securely behind us. I nod. I know all too well how carefully I must tread around this court. "Bishop Gardiner might still be in France, but he has spies everywhere who will do his bidding. The Lord Chancellor, Thomas Wriothesley, is one of his people and he has been keeping a keen watch on you."

"What?" I ask, stunned. "How do you know?"

Anne shrugs. "I have been at this court long enough to have eyes and ears everywhere," she says calmly.

"He has a spy?" I ask, nearly breathless. "Among my ladies?"

Again she shrugs. "We cannot have Anne Askew in your rooms again" is all she will say.

"Nan," I say grabbing her hands. "Will they hurt her?"

"Anne?" she asks, and I nod.

She shrugs again and I want to shake her in frustration. "Katie," she says to me, her voice calm. "Everyone at court knows your reformist leanings. Even if none of your ladies has said anything, it is plain for the gentlemen of the king's privy chamber to see where your allegiance lies."

"How?" I ask, somewhat mystified.

"Are you going to tell me that when you go to see the king each night and converse with him that you do not debate with him? Sir Anthony has told Joan all about your lively religious discussions with the king." I feel the blood drain from my face. Joan Denny is one of my ladies and her husband, Sir Anthony Denny, is first gentlemen of the king's privy chamber and keeper of the privy purse. He is often with the king when I go to see him, but I have given little heed to his presence when I engage in theological discussion with my husband.

"Do not think, Kate," Anne says gently, "that because he made you regent in his absence and because he entrusts the care of his children to you that you can lower your guard around him. He is a king who does not like to be crossed and he is a king who does not like a wife who is smarter than he. He loved Jane Seymour because she was quiet and compliant, he allowed Anne of Cleves a reprieve because she was willing to be put aside without a fight, but do not forget what he did to the wives who were loud and outspoken in their opinions. One he divorced and banished to die in a cold castle and the other he beheaded on Tower Hill. It will not be your reformist leanings that will kill you as much as your desire to outsmart the king."

"I have no desire to outsmart the king!" I gasp. "Only to engage in discussion."

"Kate, he doesn't want a smart wife, just a compliant one."

"Then why did he make me regent? Why would he leave me in charge of the entire realm while he went out to fight?"

"He didn't leave you to be regent alone," she points out. "He left some of his best counsellors with you. Besides, that had nothing to do with how you made him appear. Henry hates to appear weak or foolish and an overly smart wife who likes to talk will do just that."

When she leaves me, I am shaken. I have been so certain of my place at court, my place in the king's affections, that I have not for a moment thought that I could ever be in danger. But then I realise that nothing is ever certain with this king. He may be merry when he breaks his fast and murderous when he takes his lunch, and no-one can know for certain what made the difference.

Summer, 1546

They have been killing and imprisoning reformists since Stephen Gardiner arrived home from France. He returned in spring and now summer is upon us and things are getting worse. The king has also been foul tempered of late and there have been terrible rumours that he means to take another wife. Worse still, we hear that he means to have Katherine Brandon, Duchess of Suffolk, as his seventh wife. I am appalled—as is she. Her husband, Charles Brandon, died last summer and Henry grieved most of all. That he would think to cast his eye on his best friend's widow so soon after his death shocks me.

So when I find myself once more at Whitehall Palace, I cannot take pleasure in watching the meadow larks frolic on the banks of the river or in ordering new shoes or even in eating my favourite sweet pastries. I find that the only comfort I have is in reading my Bible and immersing myself in my writing. I am writing a book and it is to be called *The Lamentation of a Sinner*. I have been working on it for quite some time and I had hoped to have it published, but now I am wary of what trouble it might cause.

The translation of *Psalms and Prayers* that we worked on in my rooms was published just last year by the royal printer, Thomas Berthelet, and I am also engaged in translating Erasmus' *Paraphrases upon the New Testament* from Latin into English. I feel that this will be my most significant work for Erasmus' Latin version is exquisite and I long to make it available in English. I have convinced Princess Mary to help me in this endeavour and she is translating the gospel of John, while I translate the gospel of Matthew. We have been working on this project for almost a year and I have loved every moment of it.

But I fear my scholarly pursuits and my study of the Scriptures have made me more opinionated and combative. I have had more discussions with my husband the king and I sense, slowly, that my sister has been right all along. He does not want an intelligent wife, merely a compliant one, and now with all the rumours swirling around me, I begin to fear for my life.

I keep myself busy throughout the day with my work. My rooms are always buzzing with readings or sermons or translations in progress, but I feel a sense of tension rising throughout the court. The king's health is rapidly declining and he is more irritable and petulant than usual. Everyone can sense that the end is near, though no-one dares to say it out loud. Imperceptibly, factions spring up at court. There are the Seymours and others like them who are reform minded, and then there is Stephen Gardiner and men like Thomas Wriothesley and Richard Rich, who are eager for an opportunity to throw out the reformists and re-establish the old religion. Amid all of this, my little Edward continues to grow into a strong reformist prince.

And then without warning, like a striking snake, all hell breaks loose around us. I am in my rooms in the afternoon, working on my translation of the gospel of St Matthew when my brother sweeps in. I am shocked to see him, for I had not expected him.

"Your Highness," he bows low before me, and I incline my head and motion for him to rise.

"Would you join us, Lady Pembroke?" I ask, nodding at my sister.

I instruct my ladies to continue with their work and then lead my siblings into my privy chamber and shut the door.

"What is it?" I ask. "What has happened? Why have you come to me in the middle of the day unannounced?"

"They have taken Anne Askew," William says grimly, and I reach out to grasp the chair beside me.

"Good heavens," Anne murmurs. "When?"

"I have just been with the Privy Council. She has been brought to Greenwich to answer charges."

"What charges?" I ask. "Who has brought her in?"

"Gardiner has brought her to clarify her views on the sacrament."

The blood drains from my face and I sit down in my chair. "Gardiner wants her put to death?"

"No, Kate," he says quietly. "Gardiner wants you put to death."

"Me?" I ask in disbelief. "But what have I to do with Anne Askew?"

"She was here in your rooms last year, was she not?"

I glance nervously at Anne and I nod. "But it was just to discuss Scripture and hear her speak, Will. We didn't speak about any topics that have been proscribed by the king and it was in broad daylight. It is not as though we were doing anything in secret!"

He shakes his head and paces before me. "Did you speak of the mass?" he asks.

"No, of course not. We steered clear of that topic, knowing how strongly the king feels about it."

"What has she said?" Anne interrupts.

Will runs a hand through his hair and sighs. "She has not incriminated anyone, if that's what you're asking," he says, his gaze darting between Nan and me.

She nods. "Have they asked? For names that is? Have they asked her to name anyone?"

I stare at Anne in shock. "Why would they do that?"

"Kate, they are aiming to have you killed," she says plainly. "You are too outspoken and too reformist in your views. And you have made Prince Edward, the heir apparent, just as reform minded as you are. They need to get rid of you and find a new queen." Anne is calm, as though she is explaining all this to a child, and I remember that she has seen this scenario play out before.

"What should I do?" I ask.

"Lay low," William says. "Do nothing that will compromise you in any way."

I think about this for a moment and then I say, "I will still continue my translations and we will still continue our afternoon discussions."

William hesitates. "Kate," he says. "Perhaps…"

I shake my head and cut him off. "No," I say, "I am doing nothing wrong. Everyone knows that I have been working on Erasmus' paraphrases and everyone knows that we study the Scriptures together in my rooms. I will merely be careful about whom I invite."

I begin to hear reports that many of the preachers we have had in my rooms have been arrested. Master Hugh Latimer, who we have heard on several occasions, is taken, as is Rowland Taylor, a close associate of Dr Cranmer. We are fearful, but I refuse to be cowed, especially not by the likes of Stephen Gardiner.

But then we hear reports that are more terrifying than we have ever imagined. Anne Askew is brought before the Privy Council and Stephen Gardiner himself privately urges her to recant. He makes every effort to trap Mistress Askew, but she is calm and unwavering before him. She is removed from Greenwich to Newgate Prison, where she falls ill but still she remains unwavering in her faith. She will not recant. She will not deny her faith. I am both inspired and terrified by her conviction. Daily, I wait for news about her. Mistress Askew's faith and determination drive me onwards in my work of translation. I am determined to produce a flawless translation of Erasmus' work so that more people may have the Bible in English.

Then we receive news that Mistress Askew has been brought to the Tower of London to be interrogated by Lord Chancellor Thomas Wriothesley and Sir Richard Rich. They are merciless and cruel beyond belief and do what has never been done before—they place her on the rack. We are all appalled, for it is unheard of for a gentlewoman to be racked in the Tower of London.

"They have racked her for a reason," Anne whispers to me.

"Of course!" I sputter. "They have racked her because they hope she will recant."

"No," Anne shakes her head, "they have racked her because they hope that she will name other women who are reformist minded, namely women within the queen's rooms."

I stare at my sister in horror. "Nan, are you sure? Who has told you this?"

"It does not matter where it has come from, only that it is reliable. As they racked her, they asked her about Katherine Brandon, Joan Denny and Anne Seymour." Anne's voice is without emotion. I begin to tremble and sink weakly into a nearby chair. These are all ladies who are close to me, ladies whose husbands serve in the king's privy chamber.

"They want to brand us all as heretics? Do they not know that all we do is read our Bibles and listen to sermons and that the king himself knows it?"

"They do not care if we read the Bible from morning till noon. What they do care about is if we believe in justification by faith or if we denounce the mass. If we breathe even a word of this, they have cause against us all."

They burn Mistress Askew at Smithfield as a heretic. She is too weak to walk after being on the rack, and they have to carry her to the stake in a chair and tie her to keep her upright. We mourn the passing of our sister and will not forget her.

We move from Whitehall to Greenwich Palace. Perhaps Mistress Askew's death has emboldened me, but I find that instead of backing down, I am debating with my husband more vociferously than ever. My sister keeps cautioning me to be still and I sense that the net is tightening around me, but I cannot help myself.

Gardiner is watching me and he will use anything I give him to see me fall, so I take necessary precautions. I summon my uncle, Sir William Parr of Horton, to court and ask him to take possession of some of my books. The king has issued a proclamation against heretical writings and my sister and I go through my books and pack away everything that has even a whiff of what the king deems as heresy. We load them into trunks, strap them and give them to my uncle to take with him to the north for safe keeping. We are determined to not give Gardiner anything to use against us.

I go down to my husband's room every night before supper to visit with him. Tonight, I find him in particularly jovial humour and we engage in a lively discussion. I soon forget that we are surrounded by the gentlemen of his chamber; indeed, I even forget that Stephen Gardiner himself is seated beside my husband. Suddenly, after I have made a particularly good point, my husband turns away from me and says loudly to Stephen Gardiner, "A good hearing it is when women become so learned, and a great comfort to me in my old age to come to be taught by my wife!"

I could not be more shocked if he had reached out and struck me across the face. I blanch and begin to feel lightheaded. Gardiner's beady eyes shift to me, a smug smile on his face. He then leans close to my husband and whispers in his ear. Imperceptibly, I feel the balance of power shift and a cold shiver begins to snake up my spine. When I go back to my rooms after dinner, I tell my sister what has happened and I see that she is visibly shaken.

"You must be prepared for the king to act," she tells me quietly. "Prepare yourself to be caught unawares, for he often strikes without warning."

I do not understand why we are back at Whitehall in the height of summer. It is conveniently close to the Tower and I am nervous.

"Have you heard anything?" I ask Anne, when she comes in to help me undress one night. She shakes her head, working at the laces on my sleeves.

"I have heard nothing—which makes me very nervous," she murmurs.

"All anyone needs to do is come into my rooms at night, arrest me and whisk me away in an unmarked barge down to the Tower and no-one will know," I say with a nervous laugh.

"Exactly," Anne says, her voice quiet and grim, "and I would not put it past the king to do exactly that."

There is a quiet tap on my door and I start. Anne and I stare at each other, our faces white with terror. Motioning for me to say nothing, Anne moves to the door, opens it and slips outside. I hear muffled voices and then the door opens once more and my sister enters.

"Who is it?" I ask.

"Dr Wendy," she says quietly.

"The king's physician? What has happened? Is the king unwell?"

Anne shakes her head. "Kate," she says, then hesitates as though she cannot find the words she needs.

"Nan, you're scaring me. What is it?"

She stares steadily at me. "Dr Wendy would like to speak to you."

"Now?" I ask, looking down at myself. I am half undressed and about to prepare for bed.

"You should see him," she adds. I hesitate only for a moment before nodding. "Very well, help me with my sleeves." She deftly re-laces my sleeves and repins my hood.

When I go out into my presence chamber, Dr Wendy is pacing like a nervous cat.

"Dr Wendy," I say, and he jumps, turns around and bows low.

"Your Highness," he murmurs.

"Lady Pembroke informs me that you would like to speak to me?"

"Your Highness," he says, his eyes darting over his shoulder to the double doors at the entrance to my presence chamber. "I fear I have most disturbing news." He thrusts a single sheet of paper towards me and I snatch it up and unfold it. At first I am not sure what I am seeing but as the meaning of the words begins to become clear, I start to tremble violently.

"What is it?" Anne asks, and I give her the paper.

"It is a bill of articles against me, signed by the king himself. They mean to arrest me."

"I fear that is not all, your Highness," Dr Wendy says quietly. "They mean to search your rooms to see if they can find anything that would implicate you in being engaged in extreme reformist activities. And they mean to question your ladies, Lady Pembroke being one of them." Beside me, Anne gasps.

"Where did you get this?" I ask Dr Wendy, motioning towards the paper in my sister's hand.

"It was...dropped by the way, by one of the king's privy councillors. The rest of the information I have heard from the king himself. They mean to move against you, your Highness."

When I hear these words, it is as though a thread within me snaps. A tide of images rushes into my mind. I imagine Queen Katherine of Aragon beseeching the king on bended knee, pleading with him before the court to preserve their marriage. I imagine the beguiling Anne Boleyn laying her slender neck to the block before the hooded executioner. I imagine Jane Seymour's terrified cries, calling for her husband after the birth of her child, only to find that he has left her to die alone. I see Katherine Howard laying her neck to the block. Am I to be next—the third queen to have her head chopped off in front of a crowd of spectators on Tower Green? Am I to be another tragic wife of King Henry VIII, as I feared at the beginning?

My knees buckle beneath me and I begin to cry hysterically. It is too much. I cannot think of it. I hear footsteps rushing into my chamber and then gentle hands bearing me up and carrying me to my bed. I am beside myself with fear. Once I am settled in my bed, my sister dismisses everyone and shuts the door behind them.

"Kate," she says quietly, sitting beside me. When I do not cease my sobbing and wailing, she grabs my shoulders and shakes me. "Katherine! Stop it now!"

I draw in a deep shuddering breath and look up at her. "He will kill me," I say in a crazed whisper. "He will chop off my head like he did Katherine Howard and Anne Boleyn." I give a hysterical little laugh. "Two Katherines beheaded, one after another."

"Kate, it isn't done yet." She is quiet for a moment. "You have at least been warned of what is coming so you will not be caught unawares."

"A fat lot of good that will do me," I say shuddering. "How now, my lords," I say sarcastically. "I had not expected you to come for me during this hour of the night. I had thought you would wait till breakfast."

"You need to go to the king and change his mind."

"Have you lost your wits, Nan? Do you not remember what he did to Queen Katherine? She knelt before him, before an entire chamber of lords, and begged him not to cast her aside and did he listen? No! He flung her aside and married Anne Boleyn. Why do you think he would give ear to me?"

"Because he is old and feeble. Because he already has an heir. Because he is fond of you," she stands and whirls away from the bed and begins to pace. "This is not his doing alone," she says.

I scramble into a sitting position and look at her, my eyes wild. "Gardiner?" I whisper.

"Yes. He has wanted to be rid of you for some time. He does not like the influence you have over the king and the crown prince, but he has not had any reason to have you tossed aside before. But now he does. I believe you have angered the king by all your debating."

I take a deep breath and nod. She is right. I have not known my place. "So what do I do now?" I ask. "They have an elaborate plan to get rid of me."

"But no proof," she says.

"They do not need proof, Nan. They will manufacture it. Think of what Wriothesley and Richard Rich did to Mistress Askew."

"And yet she breathed not a word against any of us."

"Well, that will not stop them. They will fabricate something and the king will back them. All so he can make me know my place."

There is a commotion outside my door and I hear the king's voice, loud and booming. "Where is she? Where is my Kate? I heard that she has fallen ill!"

Anne gasps and I scramble back underneath the covers, just as the door to my privy chamber bursts open and the king limps in. He is leaning heavily upon the shoulder of a miserable-looking page and fills the doorway with his large frame. As he stands there, tall and broad and imposing, his beady eyes looking over me, I find myself trembling once more. My life is in the hands of this feckless, tyrannical man and there is nothing I can do about it.

"Ah, Kate," he says, covering the distance between the door and my bed with laboured steps. "Is it true that you were taken ill?"

"Yes, Your Majesty," I say meekly.

My face is so pale and my limbs so weak that it is not a lie. I am sick with fear. He stays with me for an hour, talking to me, comforting me. The picture of a good husband. And the longer he stays the more unhinged I become, for I cannot fathom what kind of man could treat his wife so solicitously one moment while plotting to imprison and kill her the next. "Oh, lord husband," I suddenly burst out sobbing. "I fear that I have displeased you."

Anne shoots me a startled glance and even I am shocked at my outburst, but I cannot help it. I am terrified.

"There, there," he soothes me. "You have not displeased me, dear Kate."

Instead of calming me, his manner only agitates me more because it confirms to me just how two-faced he is. He stays with me for another hour, soothing me whenever I start to sob again. Finally, when he is gone, Anne comes to sit beside me. "You are going to have to pull yourself together and come up with a plan," she tells me firmly, "or we will all lose our heads."

I can barely sleep that night and I spend much of it in prayer, pleading with God for wisdom. There is something about coming face to face with death that jolts you awake as nothing else can. I find that I am taking careful stock of who I am, what I want and what I am willing to die for. Were I in Mistress Askew's position, racked and asked to recant on pain of death, what would I do? I wrestle with this question all night. Is God calling me to sacrifice myself for my faith? Could I bear to? Could I bear not to?

When dawn streaks the sky, Anne comes into my chamber. "Katie," she says to me, seeing what a state I am in. "Have you not had any sleep?"

I shake my head. My eyes are red-rimmed and I still feel a trace of wild irrational hysteria. "What should I do?" I ask her, as she comes to stand beside me.

"You must go and convince him that you do not mean to teach him. That you know your place and that you will not rise above it."

"How?" I ask.

"I think that you must try to convince him that you have only sought to debate with him as a diversion. To take his mind off his ailments. Never to instruct him and never to reveal your own opinions." I consider this for a moment. "Frankly, I do not think he cares much what you believe, so long as you bow the knee to him."

"So I need not recant?"

"No, I think not. If you are careful, you will never back yourself into that corner. If you do this right, you will win his favour, keep your head atop your neck and still continue to be an unapologetic reformist. Let us not give Gardiner what he wants."

I stare at Anne absently, my mind already beginning to form the speech that I will give to Henry. "Not give Gardiner what he wants?" I ask.

"Yes," she replies. "He wants your head on a platter. And we will not give that to him."

I spend much of the day in prayer. We continue our Bible readings in the afternoon, as though nothing has happened, but there is a palpable tension in my rooms. Everyone is afraid of what will happen next. Rumours are rife about court of preparations being made for my arrest, of the Lord Chancellor Thomas Wriothesley having been commissioned to arrest me when I least expect it. I keep my head high and pray as though my life depends upon it, for it does. It is no longer a net that I feel tightening around me but a noose.

That evening I take care with my dress, then with my sister and my cousin Maud I make my way to the king's chambers as I always do. I find him sitting amid his gentlemen and there is a hush when I enter the room.

"My lord husband," I say, curtseying low. "Good health to you."

He bids me rise and I take my place beside him. The room is so quiet that the silence is stifling. Without warning, Henry begins to talk about religion. At first I think that I have misheard him. He launches into a lively discussion of some Bible topic and my mind ticks over the plans that I have formulated all day. "And what think you, my dear Kate?" he asks, conversationally, turning to me and watching me with his beady eyes.

I take a deep breath and launch into my rehearsed response. It is a response I have prepared all day, a speech so sickly sweet that I fear we might all choke on it. "Since God has appointed such a natural difference between man and woman, and Your Majesty is so excellent in gifts of wisdom and I, a silly woman, so much inferior in all respects of nature to you, how comes Your Majesty to inquire my judgment in such causes of religion?" I hold my breath, watching him.

"Not so, by St Mary," he snaps. "You are as learned as a doctor, Kate, qualified to instruct us and not be directed by us."

I then launch into a lengthy and impassioned assurance that this has not been my desire at all. I assure him that I long to be instructed by a husband as wise and virtuous as he and that I have only tried to converse with him in such a lively way to help occupy his mind.

He seems pleased by my assertions and exclaims, "And is it even so, sweetheart, my dear Kate? And tended your arguments to no worse end than to distract me from my pain? Then perfect friends we shall be."

And just like that, all is forgotten. There has been no logical discussion between grown adults. So long as we all tell Henry that we will not cross him and do exactly as he says, he is happy. It is as though we are in the royal nursery and Henry is lord of it all, refusing to allow his will to be crossed. It is as simple as that. He is a king who will not allow anyone to cross him.

I make my escape unscathed, yet I have no inkling of what is still to come.

The next day I am seated with the king beside the river, taking the air and watching the birds flit across the pure blue sky, when I see Sir Thomas Wriothesley approaching us. My pulse quickens, for I see that he has with him forty armed men. The king sits up as they approach. I suddenly realise that they are coming to arrest me. I can see it from the grim set of Sir Thomas' jaw and the triumphant gleam in his eye. I fear that I am about to faint, when suddenly the king rises to his feet and bellows, "Away fool! Away arrant knave!"

I see Sir Thomas blanch and stop so abruptly that his guards barely escape crashing into him. "Your Majesty," he blubbers. "We are here to arrest..."

"Arrest!" the king shouts. "Who are you here to arrest?"

"Your Majesty...we...that is...I thought...the queen." Sir Thomas cannot seem to string together a single coherent sentence.

"Away! Do you dare impugn the honour of my queen before my very face?"

None of us knows how to react. Finally, Sir Thomas and his men slink away, confused and embarrassed, and the king sinks down beside me with a self-satisfied smirk on his face. "There, there, my beautiful Kate," he says soothingly. "You have nothing to fear. I shall protect you."

Later in my rooms I hear that the king chose not to tell Sir Thomas that he changed his mind about my arrest after the speech the night before. He wanted to make sure that even Sir Thomas knew his place.

He is mad, I think. *He will stop at nothing to get his own way.* I decide then that I will keep my head low and continue to immerse myself in what matters most to me: my study of the Scriptures and raising Edward and Elizabeth as reformists. I will devote myself to these things so that one day, when history tells my story, I will be remembered as the queen who studied Scripture and encouraged others to do the same. Henry may have played me for a fool and forced me to deny my intelligence, but he will not have the last word. I will educate his heirs to be true reformists and through them I will influence England for the cause of reform. I will be remembered as England's first truly reformist queen.

Windsor, England
February 16, 1547

I am seated in my private chapel, the queen's closet, within St George's Chapel. My face is composed, my hands primly folded on my lap. My sister Anne is seated beside me. I am dressed in blue velvet, the colour of royal mourning. The last time a queen outlived her husband was when Queen Elizabeth Woodville laid her husband King Edward IV to rest. They were Henry's maternal grandparents. Since that time, every King of England has outlived his queen. Henry himself has outlived four of his queens, but today I take my place beside Elizabeth Woodville, a dowager queen in mourning.

The king died in the small hours of January 28. I am told he did not suffer. I am told he called Thomas Cranmer, his reformist friend, to hear his last confession. I am told he held Dr Cranmer's hand as he died. Now we are here to watch as the king is interred beside his most beloved wife, Queen Jane, the only woman who managed to give him what he longed for most: a son and heir.

I cannot believe that I have outlived him. Of all his wives, it is I who have survived. I have not been the most outspoken, the most courageous or even the most foolish, yet I have survived. And now what will I do? I have so many things that I want to accomplish, but perhaps the most significant thing I will do is to finally publish my books. I will publish my own work, *The Lamentation of a Sinner*, and my translation of Erasmus' *Paraphrases upon the New Testament* in English. I have kept them hidden for fear of the king, but now that I have survived, I will release them into the world so that others might benefit from them.

With Henry's death, a new day has dawned for England. My beloved little prince, Edward, is to be crowned a few days from now, then England will truly be a reformist kingdom. He will bring in changes and open doors that none of us have dared to imagine. I am glad I have survived to see this day and even more glad to have had a part in it. I am glad that my influence over this young boy has turned his heart to reform and the Scriptures. Regardless of the other influences that will now surround him on his journey as king, the influence I have wielded in his life as a mother will now finally come to fruition for England.

Katherine Parr (1512–1548) embraced the Reformation during her time as Queen of England. Life at court, as the sixth wife of King Henry VIII, afforded her opportunities to become acquainted with some of the brightest reformist thinkers of her time. Her translated and original works helped spread the truth she embraced throughout England and other parts of Europe and her care in educating Prince Edward and Princess Elizabeth in the reformed faith changed the religious direction of the nation. Soon after Henry VIII's death, she married Sir Thomas Seymour, but died shortly after due to complications following the birth of her first and only child, Mary Seymour.

8

Katherine Brandon

FAR FROM THE BURNING SHORE

Lincolnshire, England

Spring 1554

The sheriff of Lincolnshire brings the rain with him. Thick silver ropes that pummel the damp earth around Grimsthorpe Manor and send the magpies and starlings twittering into the trees in search of cover. I do not even know that he has come until my husband strides into the nursery, where I am cooing over our newborn daughter, his face grim.

"I have need of you, my dear," he says without preamble.

"What has happened?" I ask, hurriedly handing Susan to her nurse, Margaret Blackburn, and walking towards my husband. He gently takes my arm and leads me out of the nursery and into the hallway outside.

"The sheriff of Lincolnshire is here," he says, and my hand flies to my mouth. "Why? Who is he here for?"

"He says he has a warrant for my arrest," Richard says, and immediately I feel my knees begin to buckle beneath me. Richard's grip on my elbow tightens and he anchors me against his side.

"No!" I say. "Oh, dear God, no! Why? Why does he want to arrest you? Is there anyone else with him? Did you see? Are they to take you to the Tower?" My mind is whirling with possibilities and I can't seem to get a grip on my emotions.

"Katherine," he says, gently. "Kit, look at me." I look up into his eyes and he smiles. "It is not all that bad. I do not think that they mean to take me to the Tower."

I shake my head. "You do not know that. You do not know what Queen Mary will do, not with that man sitting at her right hand and whispering in her ear."

Richard takes a deep breath and nods. "You are right. But even Stephen Gardiner is not so bold or so foolish as to attack you like that."

"No," I concede. "Perhaps not. What does the sheriff say?"

Richard narrows his eyes. "I have asked him to wait in the great hall while I bring you in. He has only told me he has a warrant for my arrest. I thought that it would be wise to have you there while he reads out the charges and goes into all the details."

I nod and pull myself upright. "Yes, yes, that is wise," I nod. "I will come directly." Richard loosens his grip on my elbow but does not release me.

Together we make our way through the maze of hallways and galleries towards the great hall on the ground floor. Grimsthorpe has been my home all my life. It was given to my father, Baron Willoughby, as a gift by King Henry VIII on the occasion of my parents' marriage. At that time, my mother was Queen Katherine of Aragon's chief lady-in-waiting and much beloved by both the king and the queen.

When we reach the great hall, I see the sheriff and another man standing together, shifting uncomfortably. I sweep into the room and arrange my face carefully into my most imperious expression.

"How now, good sirs. To what do we owe the pleasure of this visit?"

They bow at my greeting. I am still the dowager Duchess of Suffolk and they acknowledge me as such.

"Your grace," they murmur deferentially, before turning to my husband with a nod. "Master Bertie."

"And why are you here?" I ask.

The sheriff clears his throat and scratches his head. "Well, my lady, we are here to arrest Master Richard and bring him with us, without bail, to London."

I feel faint when they mention London, but I manage to cling to my composure. "Who has ordered this?" I ask.

"The Lord Chancellor, your grace, Bishop Gardiner."

The blood drains from my face when I hear this. *The old snake!* I think.

"And what are the charges, sheriff?"

"Well, it says here," he pulls out a scrap of paper and surveys its contents, "that Master Bertie is to be held in contempt for ignoring two previous subpoenas, issued by the bishop."

"Subpoenas? I have received no subpoenas," Richard says in surprise. "And, at any rate, what was I was being subpoenaed for?"

The sheriff shrugs. "Doesn't say. Only that you are to be arrested and brought to London."

I am seething inside and feel as though I could wring Gardiner's neck if he were standing before me now. I stare the sheriff down until he squirms and says, "But seeing as how you are a trustworthy squire, Master Bertie, and your grace is well acquainted with Her Majesty the Queen, I do not think it necessary for Master Bertie to be dragged into London like a common malefactor. Perhaps if he were to post bail? I would be willing to release him if you were to produce bail of a thousand pounds? Provided, of course, that he would present himself to the Lord Chancellor in London, no later than Good Friday coming."

I am about to open my mouth to object, determined not to play into Gardiner's hands, when Richard says calmly, "That sounds reasonable." I stare at him like he has gone mad.

"Ah good. Yes, very good then." The sheriff looks relieved. Obviously he has expected more of a fight, especially from me.

"Go down to the kitchens and see to some bread and drink for yourselves," Richard says. "My lady and I will confer and have the bail bonds brought to you shortly."

"Very good, Master Bertie." The sheriff is now all smiles and affable charm. With one more bow to me, they retreat.

I am about to open my mouth to protest when Richard shakes his head and grabs my arm. He propels me into the steward's room, sends the man to make the bail arrangements with the sheriff, then shuts the door behind him.

"You cannot be serious!" I burst out when we are alone. "This is a ploy! A ruse to lure you into London so he can fabricate some foolish charge and lock you up in the Tower!"

"No," Richard shakes his head, "I do not think so. For if it were as easy as that, Gardiner would have already sent a small contingent from London to take me. He would not have used the sheriff of Lincolnshire to do it."

I sigh. "We do not know what he is thinking. And now that I am no longer at court, I have no influence whatsoever."

He shrugs. "It is not as though you would have an influence at all given our current circumstances."

I have to agree to this. We are at our lowest point in royal favour. Queen Mary is Romanist, decidedly so, and I am equally reformist. To make matters worse, my family—that is the family of my deceased husband, the Duke of Suffolk—was recently at the centre of one of the most treacherous plots to seize the throne in a long time. Quick-witted Queen Mary managed to raise her standard at Framlingham and march into London to claim her throne, but the pretender, my step-granddaughter Lady Jane Grey, has been beheaded, as has her father and a whole host of other peers of the realm. My step-daughter Frances, the queen's own cousin, has been spared and is even now at court trying to win back royal favour. It is a terrible debacle and I have been here, hidden away in Lincolnshire, trying to lay low and stay clear of it all.

"They hate reformists," I blurt out, and Richard, who has been standing at the windows staring out at the rain, turns to face me.

"Yes," he agrees. "And we are some of the staunchest reformists in the realm. But, of late, the queen has been too busy beheading the traitors who tried to steal her throne and so we are safe."

"For the time," I say bitterly. "I am sure Gardiner will find a way to accuse me of something."

"Perhaps," Richard concedes. "Which is why I need to go to London and see what he wants. I doubt that he will try to arrest me in London, Kit. It will do him no good. The queen has no reason to suspect you of treason."

"No," I say, "she does not. Even if she had, I *think* she would at least spare me for the love that our mothers had for each other. And the queen loved my mother as well." I sigh. "Do you see no other way to handle this? Can we not leave?"

"The country?" he asks me, and I nod. Richard shakes his head. "No, well, not right now at any rate. If we were to leave, it would have to be well thought out and I would need to spend some time away, perhaps in the Low Countries, organising it all. We cannot just up and leave." He purses his lips and is silent for a moment. "No, Katherine, our best bet is to see what Gardiner wants. Let him think that we have played into his hands for now and then surprise him. We have no other option."

I sink into the nearest chair suddenly feeling very weary. I can see that we are standing at the beginning of a long and dangerous game, and I do not have the foresight to see which of us will win.

Richard leaves for London on the morrow. After breakfast and time with my daughter, I take myself down to the stables and have the groom saddle my horse. I need to think, and the best way I can do that is on a long ride through the beautiful countryside I have known since I was a young girl.

As I ride through the open fields, the cold wind stinging my cheeks and the clean scent of damp earth filling my nostrils, I mull over my life. Sometimes, when you see giants looming ahead, it is good to look back and take stock of where you have come from. To remember how God has led you in the past so that you can have courage to face whatever lies in the future.

I feel as though I have lived three lifetimes. The first and most precious was as the only daughter and heiress of Baron Willoughby and his Spanish bride, Maria de Salinas. They were happy, carefree days of riding in the countryside, learning my Latin and my Greek, and dutifully praying in our private chapel each morning. I remember the feel of the rosary beads in my fingers and the faint scent of oranges that always seemed to cling to my mother, as she knelt beside me.

And then not long after my father died, I began my second life as the wife of Charles Brandon, Duke of Suffolk, the king's best friend. I was fourteen and he was forty-nine, fit to be my grandfather. A small shudder passes through me as I think of it. I cannot regret the marriage though, for he gave me my two sons, my two precious boys. But then they were all gone. Charles first, then a few years later our teenage sons died within an hour of each other of the dreaded sweating sickness, a disease so vile that a man may be merry at breakfast and dead by lunch. They were dead before I could reach them, before I could lay my cool hand on their fevered brows and kiss them goodbye. I buried my sons and it felt as though I would never rise again, like a terrible blighting wind had knocked me over. My husband was dead, my boys dead, and I was left alone.

But in the folds of my life as the Duchess of Suffolk there lies a wonderful golden thread, wound tight around my heart. As I cast about for something to hold on to, I found my Bible and in its pages I found my God. Every promise knit me to Him, weaving me together and making me whole.

I only dared explore the ideas of the reformed faith after my mother died, for she was a determined Romanist and would have burnt me alive at the stake herself had she known. But I drank it in like nectar, sitting beside King Henry's last wife, Queen Katherine Parr. We were friends. I was one of her ladies-in-waiting, part of a close inner circle who would listen to sermons by reformed preachers, tucked in the safety of the queen's rooms. Oh, those were glorious days! Even now, as I think of them, I feel a little tingle of pleasure. We studied the New Testament with meticulous care and listened to the sermons of Hugh Latimer and others like him. We drank so deeply of that fountain that we were giddy with life and always thirsty for more.

But then it all came crashing down around our ears. King Henry died and left us with his son King Edward, just nine years old. Edward loved God and the reformed faith and took up the cause of reform with fervent devotion. But six short years later, the beloved Tudor boy, for whom the king had turned all Christendom upside down, was dead. And now we all stand in the long shadow of his Romanist sister Mary Tudor—the only surviving child of Queen Katherine of Aragon—and are a hair's breadth from losing our necks.

Thinking of Queen Mary makes me think of the threat we are now facing and of Richard. Richard was my special gift from God, sent to me after my precious boys died. Our marriage caused something of a scandal at court. Richard was the steward of my household, a lowly squire, but I didn't care. My dead husband, Charles Brandon, was a spiritual changeling, following wherever his friend King Harry led, but Richard is so different. Richard loves God in a way that inspires me, that challenges me. Richard loves God in a way that makes me want to love Him more. And when we fell in love and he asked for my hand, I did not hesitate. I did not care one jot for the folly of rank. Richard was my Boaz and our little newborn daughter Susan is my Obed. Like Ruth, I am grateful for second chances.

And yet here I am on the cusp of losing it all again. When Mary Tudor came to the throne, she spoke soft words of tolerance. But I have known Mary all our lives and I know that it will not be long before she kindles fires for reformists at Smithfield. She has already opened the gates of the Tower of London to some of the best reformers in England. Hugh Latimer, Bishop Ridley, Archbishop Cranmer, men who have shaped my own faith, have already fallen victim to Mary's desire to purge the country of reform and restore the old religion in England.

For now the persecution of reformists is still muted. It is a quiet beast, bleating like a young lamb, yet I know that the lamb will soon rise up like a fire-breathing dragon and we shall feel the raging heat of its breath on our faces and our toes. Though Mary speaks tolerance, I fear that she will soon turn Smithfield into a giant funeral pyre, belching flames that will hover over London like the thick pall of death. There is no safety for us in Mary's England. Not unless we recant and I cannot recant.

Richard returns to me within a fortnight. I am so relieved to see him that I fly out of the house and into his arms as soon as he has dismounted from his horse.

He grins at me and asks, "Did you really think that Gardiner was going to send me to the Tower?" I nod, too overcome to speak. He shakes his head and leads me into the house. We go to my privy chamber and, once we have shut the door, I demand a recounting of all that has happened.

"What did he want?" I ask.

Richard takes a seat before the fire, which is burning low in the hearth. "Well…" he starts, pausing to tug off his boots and lift his stockinged feet onto a stool before the fire. "He brought before me a debt owed to the Crown by your late husband, the Duke of Suffolk."

"A debt to the Crown? That Charles owed? From when?" I furrow my brow as I tuck my feet up under me on the chair.

Richard shrugs. "He could not say from when, only that it was four thousand pounds and that, as the late Duke's executor, you are responsible to pay off the debt."

Suddenly, I remember what he is talking about and I shake my head. "But I paid that debt," I counter. "Do you not remember, Richard? During King Edward's reign? We paid it in instalments and it is done with."

Richard nods. "Just so. I vaguely remembered such a debt to the Crown and I told him so. He promised to look into it to be sure." He is silent, watching the fire.

"And?" I prompt. "Surely he did not have you arrested and brought to London to answer for an old debt that Charles owed King Henry years ago?"

Richard shakes his head slowly and turns to study me. "No, that was the excuse, but he made it clear to me that it was not his main concern."

"So, what was it?"

"Kit, he is angry at the way you have treated him and he wants to make you pay for it."

"How I have treated him!" I exclaim. "I have treated him just as he deserves."

"Katherine." He raises an eyebrow at me. "Do you know he recounted to me in detail all of your major offences against him?"

"Did he really?" I ask sarcastically. "And what did he say to you?"

"That you dressed your dog up to look like a bishop and named him Gardiner."

I bite my lip to hide a smile. It is true. I did do that. Richard sees my suppressed smile and grimaces.

"He also told me how you stood outside the Tower of London when he was imprisoned and called up at him that all the reformist lambs were now safe since he, the wolf, was locked in the tower." Richard shoots me a look. "Did you really do that?"

I nod, raising my chin a notch. "It was true." Richard chuckles and shakes his head.

"And then there was the time at a state dinner when you named him the man you loved worst in the realm, in front of an assembly of all manner of peers."

"Charles was alive then," I comment, remembering the incident. "He was appalled that I said such a thing but he said nothing to censure me."

"Yes, well, perhaps he should have. It might have saved us from this situation we find ourselves in," Richard says dryly.

"Richard!"

"Kitty, the man is on a personal crusade against you because you have treated him so poorly."

"And did he not deserve it?" I snap. "After what he did to Queen Katherine Parr? He plotted and schemed to send her to the Tower just because she was a reformist."

"And so he may well have done, but you should not have made your disdain known in so public a manner. Especially not to a man as resilient as Gardiner. He was a courtier and a Catholic bishop during King Henry's reign, a time when it was precarious to be both, and he came out of it smelling like a Tudor rose." Richard shakes his head with a rueful smile. "That alone should tell you something of the man's tenacity and duplicity. He is not a man you want as an enemy."

"I fear it is too late for that," I say, and Richard nods.

"Unfortunately you are right."

"Why, what did he say?"

"Well, he asked me if you are now as ready to set up the mass as you once were to tear it down."

"He is going to see me burned," I say quietly.

"Well, a peer of the realm cannot be publicly burned. He most likely wants to see your head chopped off on Tower Hill." I shudder at that. Richard reaches out and takes my hand in his, giving it a gentle squeeze. "Anyway, I made apologies for your past atrocious behaviour and told him that none could be coerced into acknowledging the old religion, especially after the new religion was held in such high regard during King Edward's reign. Then he asked me if you might be persuaded to change your mind."

I stare at him wide-eyed. "What did you say to that?"

"I said that you are a reasonable woman who could be persuaded to listen to arguments in favour of the old religion."

"Richard!" I exclaim.

He holds up his free hand in a placating gesture. "I needed to buy time. Which is exactly what I did." Richard is silent for a moment and then he says, "You know what he said to me before I left?"

"What?" I ask, not sure that I want to hear.

"He said, 'It will be a marvellous grief to the Prince of Spain, when he comes to England to marry the queen, to find within the realm a Spanish noble lady who has abandoned the old faith.'"

"He did not say that!" I say shocked.

Richard chuckles and nods. "Yes, a final hurrah in the form of a veiled threat. You are the only member of the nobility who is half Spanish and no longer a Romanist. You will stick out quite conspicuously when Prince Philip of Spain comes."

I imagine Queen Mary and Prince Philip standing before me and suddenly see myself through their eyes, as a turncoat, a traitor to the old religion. My mother would see me the same way. "I had thought that the queen's love for my mother might keep me safe," I say quietly. "But perhaps she will use it as justification to behead me."

"And me beside you. Though not being a peer of the realm, I shall be taken out and burned at Smithfield like the commoner I am."

I shake my head at him and frown. "That is not funny."

"No, my dearest, it is not. Especially not, since you have been sending money to Master Latimer and Bishop Ridley in the Tower to help ease the rigours of their imprisonment."

All the blood drains from my face as he mentions that. I had not thought of that at all.

"If the queen or Gardiner were to catch wind of *that*, they would send a contingent to arrest us without further delay and we would find ourselves in the Tower," Richard continues.

"Do you have a plan?" I ask.

He turns to me and nods slowly, "Yes, I have a plan."

London, England
Winter, 1555

Richard sends word to me at the Barbican, my London home, that we are to leave London and make our way to Tilbury where we will find refuge with a country squire. He promises to meet us there and take us to Gravesend, where we will take ship and go to the coast of Zeeland. From there, we will travel through the Low Countries to the Duchy of Cleves—and safety.

Soon after his meeting with Stephen Gardiner last year, Richard left England to make arrangements for our escape under the pretence of paying back a debt that my late husband and I owed to

Emperor Charles V. I moved with my household from Grimsthorpe to London to wait for him to send for us. So we have been waiting. I have stayed quietly at home, away from court, and I have not been sent for either.

Perhaps it is the flood of Spaniards in London on account of the queen's new husband, but I dream of my mother on the night of my departure. I see her standing on the prow of a great Spanish ship, the wind whipping around her face and the sky above her lined with black clouds. Beside her is her beloved friend and mistress, Katherine of Aragon. They stand together, hands clasped, eyes scanning the horizon, steadying each other against the heaving waves beneath them. All around them there are shouts and cries as sailors rush madly across the deck. The storm is coming. They can see it. The last storm forced them to abort their mission, pushing them back to the Spanish coast. This time they cannot go back. They must go forward. To England.

In my dream, I find that I am standing on the deck of that ship, clinging tightly to the rigging. I am making my way towards her, hand over hand. I call out to her, "Lady mother!" but the wind snatches up my words. "Lady mother!" I call again. "Mama! Mama!"

She hears me. Turns her head and smiles. I am desperate to reach her, but I don't seem to be moving. The tempest gathers momentum around us, threatening to swallow us whole. "Mama!" I call again, reaching out to her. She stands there smiling at me. I long for her blessing but I know, even in my dreams, that she would never bless the journey I am about to embark on. It goes against every fibre of her being. But it is a journey I must make. Perhaps that is why I am so desperate to reach her.

"Mama!" I call again, and she waves to me. "Be brave," she calls, and the howling wind fades away, so that all I can hear is her soft soothing voice. "Be brave, my Catalina," she says, for that is my name in her native Spanish. "Be brave, my beautiful girl."

And then she is gone and I am startled awake, my breathing shallow, my pulse racing. I take a deep breath, listening to the crackle of the fireplace, and hear a soft knock on the door of my bedchamber. One of my ladies enters silently and whispers, "It is time, your grace."

We dress in the dim light of waxy tapers, careful to make no sound. Before long, we gather in the darkness of the great hall: six of my most trusted servants, my little daughter Susan and me. Richard's servant, Robert Cranwell, has been engaged to see us to safety. As we hurry towards the front doors of my home, Susan, who is nestled tightly against my chest, gives a loud mewling wail. I try desperately to settle her, but I fear the damage has been done.

As we flee like thieves into the foggy darkness, Cranwell leading the way, I am terrified we will be caught. Richard left strict instructions that none of the servants are to know we have left till the morrow, leaving us enough time to get away in case Gardiner has planted spies in our home, which we know he is quite capable of doing.

"Your grace," Robert Cranwell says quietly, falling into step beside me. "I fear that we have awakened the household."

"Why? What have you seen?" I ask.

"It is Atkinson, your grace. He is following us."

Ducking my head, I nestle my face deeper into the folds of my hood and quicken my pace. "Are you sure?" I murmur, casting a quick sidelong glance at Cranwell.

"I am sure, your grace," Cranwell says, almost apologetically.

I force myself to think. We don't know if he is a spy but, in case he is, we must divert him so that we can slip away.

"Where is Mistress Blackburn?" I ask Cranwell, still keeping my head low. Cranwell turns and beckons for Susan's nurse, Margaret.

"Your grace?" Margaret Blackburn hurries to my side.

"Drop the package and milk pail you are holding," I instruct her.

"But your grace," Margaret protests. "These are for the babe." She looks towards the little crown of hair peeking through the top of my cloak.

"We shall have to purchase more elsewhere, but for now we need to divert Atkinson. If we don't, we may be worse off than losing a pail of milk and some clothes. Now hurry, Margaret, do as I say and drop them both."

Margaret nods. She understands the risks of being discovered prematurely. Falling back, she leaves the milk pail and the little packet of clothes in the shadows of the gate as we pass through.

Glancing back, I see the shadowy form of Atkinson stop to examine the packages, and while he is thus engaged, we slip down a foggy alley and out of his sight.

We make our way down to the Thames, which is shrouded in mist, and arrive at Lion Quay. The fog is thicker by the river, shrouding us in a gauzy mantle like spun wool. We stand shivering in the damp air, while Cranwell argues tersely with the boatman. He has arranged for a barge to take us to Tilbury but the boatman is reluctant to cast off in such thick fog.

We are all relieved when the boatman finally nods his head and beckons us aboard. We cast off into the river, gliding over the smooth surface of the water like phantoms vanishing into the mist. But we know that at dawn, if not sooner, the alarm will be raised and the phantoms will be fugitives, hunted for their heads.

Essex, England

Winter, 1555

When we reach Tilbury, we are greeted by the news that Gardiner has sent men to our London home. Our house has been searched and our servants questioned, our assets confiscated. The Privy Council has issued an order to search and watch for me, the dowager Duchess of Suffolk, at every port and inn in England. I am to be arrested. I am terrified that Gardiner will apprehend me. I do not know where Richard is and so I cannot send word to him. I only know that he has arranged with Cranwell to meet us here in Tilbury and that we are to wait for him.

We ride up to the house we are to stay in and clatter into the stableyard bone-weary. I am standing in the great foyer of the house when I hear the rhythmic thudding of hooves outside. A lone rider comes in hard and the grooms of the stable rush forward to meet him. I cannot see his face, for he is wearing a hood, but I would know him anywhere. He jumps from the horse and tosses his reins to the grinning lad. I rush out to meet him and throw myself into his arms.

"Richard!" I murmur, pulling away to gaze up into his familiar face. It has been six months since I last saw him and I have never been more happy to see anyone.

"Thank God you are safe," he says, pulling me back into his arms and holding me once more.

There is a discreet cough behind us and we pull apart. Richard grins at me, grabs my hand and turns to face our audience. Our host, Master Gosling, is standing on the steps above us.

"Master Gosling," Richard says. "We are indebted to you for your kindness."

"Oh indeed, Master Bertie, 'tis nothing to speak of. I owe Cranwell a favour and to be sure it is grand indeed to have the dowager duchess and yourself as my guests." The man's nipped red face is smiling merrily and he is every inch the country squire.

"And we are grateful," Richard says.

"But come, you must be weary from the journey. Come in and have a morsel to eat." Gosling motions us inside to dine in his great hall.

After dinner, we retire to our rooms and Richard holds Susan in his arms for the first time in months. "How she has grown," he marvels, running his hand over her little brown head and nuzzling her cheek.

I smile as I watch them. "She grows heavier by the day," I say.

"And you, Kit?" Richard extends a hand to me, Susan still securely tucked under his chin. I take his hand and let him draw me to his side. "Are you well? What news?"

"You must have heard that Gardiner sent men to our home in London?" I ask, and Richard nods, handing Susan to Margaret Blackburn, who has come to prepare the child for bed.

"I heard the Privy Council has issued orders to search and watch for you," he says. "Did you have safe passage here?"

I nod. "We had no major trouble."

Richard studies my face for a moment, then says, "Are you sure you want to do this, Katherine?"

I sigh. "What other options do we have? It is not just a possibility anymore. They are at this moment seeking to arrest me."

We go to the hearth and sit down in front of the fire. "Katherine, with the queen now pregnant, the line of succession will likely continue staunchly Catholic. We face the risk that England may never embrace the reformist doctrine again. We could be in exile indefinitely."

"Or she may be like her mother," I say. The words come out before I think and then I clamp my mouth shut.

Richard's eyes narrow. "You would not be so cruel, Kitty," he says.

I bite my lip and shake my head. "No," I say softly. "No woman can wish such a tragedy on another woman."

I think of the stories I have heard of Queen Katherine of Aragon. A string of babies, born and placed in the Tudor cradle, only to die shortly after. I cringe as I think of her heartbreak.

"No," I say again. I could never wish such a thing for Mary, no matter how desperate I am. "God save Her Majesty and may she be safely delivered of a bonny boy for England."

"A boy who is sure to bring the Inquisition," Richard says grimly, then he considers me again. "This is a big decision, to leave behind all we have ever known to go into exile."

"And should we stay and die, Richard? And what of Susan? I have already lost two children. I cannot bear to think of losing another."

"They will not kill her," he says dryly.

"No, they will do worse," I agree. "They will make her a ward of the queen and she will be raised in the old religion. The queen would do it in memory of my mother, whom she loved so dearly. I would lose my girl and my neck if I stay."

"It is risky to leave," Richard mutters. "There are spies at every port and now that Gardiner has men watching for you, we may well be caught before we manage to leave England."

"It is riskier to stay."

"What if we were to…"

"Don't say it, Richard!" I cut him off quickly. "Don't you dare suggest that we should conform. I cannot, I *will not* recant my faith to save my neck!"

He smiles at the defiant determination in my eyes. "And such a pretty neck too. I would be loath to lose it," he says, drawing a smile from me despite the grim situation.

He takes my hand. "I would not dream of surrendering our position but sometimes I can't help but wonder if we could try to negotiate with Gardiner." He pauses and shakes his head. "Running away in the middle of winter with a child not yet a year old is not an easy task, Kitty. And I cannot imagine what our lives will be like if we do manage to cross the narrow seas."

"It may not be easy, but neither is ending up in the Tower," I say, gazing at him steadily.

He kisses my knuckles. "You are so brave, my love," he says.

"God will take care of us, Richard. Nothing can separate us from the love of God. Not Mary Tudor and her fires, nor the Spanish and their Inquisition, nor the narrow seas and whatever lies beyond them. Nothing Richard. He will not fail us. Not now in the hour of our greatest need."

He stares into my earnest face for a long moment. "I know," he says softly. "I know."

Richard manages to secure passage for us on a ship leaving Gravesend for the coast of Zeeland. Twice we set sail and twice we are driven back to the English coast by strong winds.

I think of my mother setting sail from Spain, only to be driven back by hard winds. Her words from my dream come back to me, the dream I had the night before I left London: "Be brave, Catalina." And I know, although my mother would never have blessed my journey of faith or my journey into exile, that she is right. I must be brave.

I do not have rosary beads to pass through my fingers as my mother did, but I do have scriptures stored in my mind and these now become my beads, slipping through my mind in an unending roll. God will not fail me, so I shall be brave.

We are being driven back to the coast a third time and are close to shore when Richard comes to me, his brows pinched in frustration. I am lying down on a pallet in a corner of the deck, my eyes closed, my stomach heaving and a cold sheen of sweat clinging to my brow. He sits down next to me, gently stroking my hair.

"Are you unwell, my love?" he asks. I can hear the note of alarm in his voice. I struggle to sit up and he helps me, propping me up against his side. I look up at him, somewhat apprehensively. I am not sure that he will want to hear the news I am about to deliver.

"Richard," I say, fighting hard against the impulse to vomit. "Richard, I think I am with child again."

"What?" he asks, his expression dazed.

"I am with child," I repeat slowly.

"With child?" he repeats.

I shoot him a wry smile. "I am quite certain," I tell him.

Suddenly, as the news sinks in, his face breaks into a grin and he gathers me close. "Oh, my love, that is wonderful news!" Then he scans my face for a moment, his brows coming together in a frown. "But is it quite safe do you think?"

I know what he means. Being brought to childbed in England, where we have an army of maids and midwives and nurses at our beck and call is fraught with danger. The queen herself has made provision for the throne in the event that she should not survive her own labour. But giving birth in a distant land where we are virtually unknown and alone increases the risks exponentially.

"Perhaps we should stay," he says quietly. "Perhaps we have been driven back to England for this purpose."

I shake my head firmly. "I would rather be brought to childbed and die there than recant my faith. I cannot think of it."

Richard sighs, "Katherine..."

"Richard, when Queen Katherine was dying, alone and abandoned by King Henry, my mother begged to go to her so she could attend her during the final hours of her life. The king refused, but my mother saddled her horse and made the journey to Kimbolton Castle alone, in the dead of an English winter. When she got there, they refused to let her enter the castle to see the queen, but my mother forced her way in and went to the queen's side. Queen Katherine died in my mother's arms two days later." I fall silent as I think about this story and Richard watches my face, waiting for me to make my point. "Whatever else I may be, Richard, I am determined to be loyal and indomitable in my convictions, even if that means defying a monarch, even if that means taking a treacherous journey. I cannot be unfaithful to a Friend who has been so faithful to me. I cannot deny my God."

Richard's face relaxes into a soft smile. "You are a formidable woman," he says. "Very well, I will go and find Margaret and see how Susan is faring. Will you be alright in the meantime? Can I get you anything?"

I shake my head and smile up at him. "No, my love, I shall be alright. Go and see how Susan is."

The ship has just docked in England for the third time, when Richard walks quickly back to me, his face drawn. "What is it?" I ask him wide-eyed.

He crouches down next to me and says shortly, "The Yeoman of the Guard are here."

"*The queen's guard? Here?*" Panic rises in my throat. "Susan," I breathe.

"She is safe with Mistress Blackburn," he says. "It is you they are looking for. I heard them asking after you." My heart is pounding and I try to force myself to be calm.

"We cannot possibly evade them," Richard says. "There is nowhere to go."

"But perhaps they do not know what I look like," I say slowly. Richard shoots me a dubious look. "No, think about it," I insist. "I have hardly been at court since King Edward died. I only rarely see the queen and even then I am dressed differently, in slashed sleeves and a French hood, like a dowager duchess. The Yeoman of the Guard are likely watching for a woman dressed like that, accompanied by a retinue of servants. They would never suspect either one of us dressed like this." I motion to my travel-worn clothing. At best I look like a merchant's wife and nothing more.

Richard turns to look at me. "But they know you are travelling with a child," he says.

"But she is not with me now," I reply. "Margaret can easily say that Susan is her own child. Susan would not know any different," I point out, my fears beginning to ease. "Can you get word to Margaret? Have they boarded the vessel?"

"No, they were at the quay when I saw them," Richard replies. "I will go to Mistress Blackburn and inform her of the ruse. You stay here."

I lay my head down on the pallet and close my eyes to pray. Suddenly, I hear heavy footsteps coming towards me and I open my eyes again. I feel the blood draining from my face as I gaze at two Yeoman of the Guard, armed to the teeth, dressed in their distinctive uniforms of red, white and yellow. My eyes fix on the Tudor rose emblazoned at the centre of their uniform and I desperately struggle to gather my thoughts.

"How now, my lords?" I manage to choke out, scrambling to my feet. They tower over me, taking in my travel-worn garments and simple white cap. I look nothing like a dowager duchess and I am very grateful for that.

"You will pardon us, mistress," one of them says gruffly. "We had ..."

He is cut off by Richard's loud voice from behind him. "How now, sirs, what business?"

The question has a slight undertone of indignation, but even Richard is careful to temper his tone around the Yeoman of the Guard. The men swivel around and glare at Richard.

"We are looking for the dowager Duchess of Suffolk," one of them says.

Richard delicately squeezes past them and positions himself in front of me. "And does my lady *look* like the dowager Duchess of Suffolk?" he demands, sweat forming on his brow. The guards look at me, considering his question. "She is the wife of a lowly squire, my lords, and not well to boot," Richard hurries on before they have a chance to respond.

I am silently praying they will buy into the ruse, my heart thudding in my chest. I begin to feel queasy and I swallow hard against the rising bile.

"Where are you travelling to?" one of them asks.

"We are bound for the coast of Zeeland," Richard replies.

"What business there?"

I can see Richard's mind scrambling for an answer. "Trade," he says weakly.

"Trade?" The yeoman raises an eyebrow. They are watching us, no doubt accustomed to being duped by those who wish to avoid arrest.

At that moment, whether through fear or the rocking of the boat or the rustle of the child in my womb, I do not know, I feel a warm rush surge up from my belly and into my throat. Before I can stop myself, I pitch forward and heave violently, emptying the contents of my stomach directly onto the feet of the nearest yeoman.

The man makes a horrified gasp and leaps back. My cheeks are flaming with embarrassment and poor Richard is frantically rubbing my back and eyeing the yeoman. The man's face is pale and pinched.

"I am sorry," I gasp, quickly wiping my mouth on my sleeve. "Good sir, I beg your pardon. I am so sorry."

There is a long tenuous silence, and when I sneak a peek at the guards, I find that the one who has escaped being vomited on is red and shaking with suppressed laughter. The other is busy shaking his boots. Finally, Richard excuses himself and goes off to find some rags and a bucket. By the time he returns, they have left and I have sunk down onto the little pallet we have made, dizzy and weak with relief.

When the mess has been cleaned and Richard is seated next to me, I cannot help but grin at him. "It was like a bad Greek comedy," I say, shaking my head with a soft laugh. "You would do well at the playhouse, my lord."

"Only when I am in danger of losing my wife," he says wryly.

The ship finally casts off again and we have a quiet voyage across the narrow seas. We sit side by side, huddled together against the biting wind and I wish that we did not have to make this journey in the middle of winter.

I am dozing beside Richard when I hear the shouts of the sailors and feel the rush of feet running past me. "What is it? What's happened?" I mumble, rubbing my eyes.

Richard lifts his arm from around my shoulders and helps me up. We stand against the side of the ship, our hands clinging to the rigging nearby to steady ourselves and we see it. A thin curling line rising out of the mist, purple in the dawn light.

"Land ahoy!" a sailor bellows. It is the coast of Zeeland and we are almost to our destination.

"What if they will not have us?" I suddenly ask Richard, glancing worriedly at him.

He grins at me. "I thought I was the one prone to worry," he teases.

I smile back ruefully and he slips his arm around my shoulders. "Don't worry, my love," he says softly. "God numbers the very hairs on our head. We are persecuted but not forsaken."

I look up at him, searching his calm, steady face, and I know he is right. I gaze back at the dim line of the coast of Zeeland as it draws closer. A new life, a new home awaits us. We are foreigners. We do not speak their language, we are unfamiliar with their customs, but we will learn, we will adapt, we will adopt this strange new place as our home, because we have nowhere else to go. We are refugees.

But as I think of our situation, I realise that, whatever might lie ahead, we are safe. Away from Mary's England, away from Gardiner's wrath, away from the Tower and the burning pyres of Smithfield. Far from the burning shore of our beloved England.

A wave of sadness washes over me, bittersweet and filled with longing, and I wonder if we will ever see that beautiful shore again. But the answer comes like a cresting wave and lifts my spirits. Even if we never see England again, a better shore awaits us if we are brave and faithful. I smile and turn my face to the wind and the distant call of gulls as they awake to a new dawn.

Katherine Brandon, Duchess of Suffolk, (c.1519–1580) was a lady-in-waiting to King Henry VIII's sixth wife, Katherine Parr, and influenced the religious beliefs of the queen. She was a patron of English reformers, including Hugh Latimer and Nicholas Ridley, and an outspoken advocate for the Reformation, which more often than not got her into trouble. During their exile, Katherine and her second husband Richard Bertie served as administrators of Lithuania, before returning to England when it was safe to do so. Katherine had two surviving children, Susan and Peregrine Bertie, Peregrine being named for their peregrinations in exile.

Acknowledgments

They say it takes a village to raise a child. In many ways this book has been just like a child, and it has taken a village to raise it and put it out into the world. I want to thank everyone who has been a part of my village. Without you, this book would not have been possible:

My amazing editor and best friend Lauren Webb, thank you so much for just being yourself. We've been partners on so many different projects for more than a decade, but this project has been extra special to me. Thank you for lending me your brains, your wit, your talents, your time and your prayers. This book would not be what it is without you.

Nathan Brown and the Signs Publishing team, thank you for giving me the opportunity to share these stories and a platform to make the voices of these extraordinary women heard.

Lisa Clark Diller, thank you for being so generous with your expertise. I am so grateful for the time you invested in reading and commenting on this book when it was still in the early stages of development.

Adam Ramdin, Clive Coutet and the entire Lineage team, thank you for giving me the opportunity to be a part of such a talented and dedicated group of people. This book represents the countless hours I spent researching and writing for the Lineage website, and it would not exist if you hadn't taken a chance on an obscure researcher/writer from Australia.

My mom, thank you for encouraging me to always put Jesus first and to use my talents for Him. Thank you for helping me to write my first article for *Insight* magazine. This entire journey began with that first piece.

My dad, who always bought me books every chance he got, thank you for teaching me to love books and love reading.

Nena, thank you for the encouragement, prayers and countless hours spent reading and editing my many articles, blog posts, scripts and stories.

My husband Asela, thank you for always supporting every single one of my crazy ideas. From stage management, to hauling sets, to late night pick-ups, to enduring a wife with a crazy Bible work schedule, to late night bottles and nappy changes, and finally to listening to me rant and agonise over this book. Thank you for loving me just as I am.

Finally, my two little girls, Elyse and Carys. Mama wrote this book for you, so it's safe to say you both played a big role in making it happen. I love you both and I pray that you will grow to love and serve Jesus with all your hearts.

Bibliography

Anderson, J, 2012, *Ladies of the Reformation, Volume 2*, HardPress Publishing, Miami.

Bainton, R H, 1973, *Women of the Reformation: In France and England*, Augsburg Fortress Publishers, Minneapolis.

Baldwin, D, 2015, *Henry VIII's Last Love: The Extraordinary Life of Katherine Willoughby, Lady-in-Waiting to the Tudors*, Amberley Publishing, Gloucestershire.

Childs, J, 2014, *God's Traitors: Terror and Faith in Elizabethan England*, The Bodley Head, London.

Cholakian, P F, Cholakian, R C, 2005, *Marguerite de Navarre: Mother of the Renaissance*, Columbia University Press, New York.

Culp, K A, 2010, *Vulnerability and Glory: A Theological Account*, Westminster John Knox Press, Kentucky.

D'Aubigne, J H M, 2013, *History of the Reformation in the Sixteenth Century*, Delmarva Publications, Delaware.

D'Aubigne, J H M, 2013, *History of the Reformation in the Time of Calvin*, Delmarva Publications, Delaware.

De Mornay, C, 1824, *Mémoires et correspondance de Duplessis-Mornay*.

Diefendorf, B B, 1991, *Beneath the Cross: Catholics and Huguenots in Sixteenth Century Paris*, Oxford University Press, Oxford.

Fix, A C, 2013, *The Great Courses: The Renaissance, the Reformation and the Rise of Nations*, Audible.

Foxe, J, 2011, *The Unabridged Acts and Monuments Online (1583 Edition)*, The Digital Humanities Institute, Sheffield.

Goldstone, N, 2016, *The Rival Queens*, Back Bay Books, New York.

Gregory, B S, 2013, *The Great Courses: The History of Christianity in the Reformation Era*, Audible.

Gregory, P G, Baldwin, D, Jones, M, 2013, *The Women of the Cousins War: The Duchess, The Queen and the King's Mother*, Atria Books, London.

Jardine, L, 2006, *The Awful End of Prince William the Silent: The First Assasination of a Head of State with a Handgun*, HarperCollins, New York.

Knecht, R, 2007, *The Valois: Kings of France 1328–1589*, Bloomsbury, New York.

Morata, O F, 2003, *The Complete Writings of an Italian Heretic* (Translator H N Parker), The University of Chicago Press, Chicago.

Pitts, J V, 2009, *Henri IV of France: His Reign and Age*, The Johns Hopkins University Press, Baltimore.

Porter, L, 2011, *Katherine the Queen*, Macmillan, London.

Stanford, P, 2017, *Martin Luther: Catholic Dissident*, Hodder & Stoughton, London.

Tucker, R A, 2017, *Katie Luther, First Lady of the Reformation*, Zondervan, Grand Rapids.

Tylor, C, 1893, *The Camisards: A Sequel to The Huguenots of the Seventeenth Century*, Simpkin, Marshall, Hamilton, Kent, London.

VanDoodewaard, R, 2017, *Reformation Women*, Reformation Heritage Books, Grand Rapids.

Winn, C H, Larsen, A R (Editors), 1999, *Writings by Pre-Revolutionary French Women: From Marie de France to Elizabeth Vige-Le Brun*, Routledge, Oxford.

Wylie, J A, 2015, *The History of Protestantism*, Delmarva Publications, Delaware.

Sukeshinie Goonatilleke loves a good story and has been telling them as far back as she can remember. Her first article was published in *Insight* magazine in 1998 and she regularly contributed articles to the magazine for many years after. She spent a number of years directing and producing children's and youth theatre and worked as a drama teacher in her native country of Sri Lanka. She and her husband moved to Australia in 2006.

She currently writes and curates web content for Lineage Journey and is a freelance script writer for The Incredible Journey, which are both Christian media ministries. When she isn't researching or writing, Sukeshinie is homeschooling her children or curled up in a corner with a good book. She lives with her husband and two daughters in Melbourne, Australia.